# Family Meals

Also by Michael Tucker

*Living in a Foreign Language*
*I Never Forget a Meal: An Indulgent Reminiscence*

# Family Meals

## BRINGING HER HOME

## MICHAEL TUCKER

Grove Press
*New York*

*Published simultaneously in Canada*
*Printed in the United States of America*

ISBN-13: 978-0-8021-4508-6

Grove Press
an imprint of Grove/Atlantic, Inc.
841 Broadway
New York, NY 10003

Distributed by Publishers Group West

www.groveatlantic.com

10  11  12  13    10  9  8  7  6  5  4  3  2  1

Jill and I started out writing this book together, but we decided to save the marriage instead. We love to act together; we give speeches around the country together; we're great at parties; so we thought that team writing would be a snap. But no, our rhythms in that area turned out to exist on different planets. So we adopted another strategy: I would write our story and then—chapter by painful chapter—she would read it and tell me what I did wrong. That seemed to work out just fine.

Jill—as a person and as an actor—cannot help but expose herself. It's what she does; it's what makes her so beautiful. And that is what she did during every day of the writing of this book.

I dedicate the book to her courage and her magnificent heart.

# Family Meals

# Foreword

THE WOMEN HAD NATURALLY GRAVITATED to the shady
side of the table and the men sat on the exposed side, sipping their wine and warming their bald spots in the sun. We
had been at the table for hours. The *trattoria*—an *osteria,* really,
because it has some rooms to rent—sits perched on the side
of a mountain looking out onto endless groves of olive trees
that carpet the hillsides all the way down to the Spoleto valley. It was past three in the afternoon and the summer wind
whipped the silver-green branches until they looked like a
storm at sea.

The meal had progressed in the Italian manner. First,
bottles of water—gas and no gas—were opened and pitchers
of the house wine, both white and red, were put out before
us. We had silently performed the ritual of turning our glasses
right side up so they could receive their respective liquids. It
was an instant Rorschach test to see who used the large glass
for water and who used it for wine.

Antipasto had been crostini—slices of bread, toasted and
topped variously with tomatoes and basil, garlic and oil, and,
best of all, a spread of wild mushrooms and black truffles,
which are a local specialty.

The pasta course should have been enough for lunch. We ordered all the pastas: *strangozzi,* the local noodle, with truffles;
tortellini with cream, sausage bits, and truffles; and spaghetti with

tomatoes, hot pepper, and strong, salty pecorino cheese. We feasted on them family-style as the waiter refilled the wine pitchers.

We were now finishing up a mixed grill of meats that had been brought to the table on our own little charcoal grill— to keep everything properly sizzling. Lamb chops, pork chops, sausages, and pork ribs, which, unlike their American counterparts, needed no rubs, no sauce, no mouth-numbing spices—just a little salt and onto the grill.

Our friend Joe—he and his wife, Teresa, are our neighbors and friends both in New York and in Umbria—turned to the assembled group. He held a lamb chop in one hand and his glass of red wine in the other, and a little lamb grease properly decorated his chin. He lifted his glass in a toast and said, "*Abbiamo trovato l'America.*" He was beaming.

This was a new one for me. "We found America?"

"You never heard that expression before?"

I shook my head.

"Sure," said Bruno, who was the only actual Italian among us. "It means we got lucky, we stepped in it."

"At the turn of the century," said Joe, who likes to hold forth, "when all the Italians were emigrating to America and the streets were said to be paved with gold, that phrase— *trovare l'America*—came to mean 'to win the lottery, to hit the jackpot, to manifest your happiness.'"

"They had no idea how tough their life in America was going to be," added Mayes. She's married to Bruno.

I was leaning back in my chair with my hands folded across my contented belly. My brain was pleasantly buzzed. Behind Joe I could see the view all the way down to the valley floor, backlit by the sun. Our friends around the table were the best friends you could ever find. In a little while Jill and I would make our way back down the hill to our little house for an afternoon snooze and some time to ourselves.

"*Sì,*" I said to Joe. "*Abbiamo trovato l'America.*"

# ONE

# Jet Blue

I'VE BEEN ACCUSED, BY PRIGS AND CALVINISTS—and the occasional internist—of having too much fun in my life. Or, rather, of putting too much value on having fun, as if the pursuit of pleasure isn't a proper enterprise for a grown person. I'm not here to debate the issue; you can live how you like. But I'll stand by my program of enjoying a good meal whenever I can, sipping the appropriate spirited beverages and indulging in almost anything else that brings the blood to the surface and a gleam to the eye. I couldn't do otherwise; it's my nature. My first spoken word was "menu."

This has often been a prickly point between my wife, Jill, and myself. Not that she doesn't like pleasure—she has a healthy aptitude for it, actually. But she doesn't want to *appear* as if she does. She wants to publicly blame all her pleasure on me—as if it's something she has to endure as a condition of marriage. And that's fine; I can take the hit.

This all came up on a plane trip we were taking from New York, where we now live, to Santa Barbara to visit Jill's mom, Lora. Jill had been taking a lot of these trips recently because Lora and her second husband, Ralph, were getting on in years. Lora was eighty-seven and Ralph had just achieved ninety-one. The problem was that every time Jill came home after one of these jaunts, she was stressed and depleted and it took me days just to scrape her off the floor. Her mother always managed to put her into this state. And apparently it's been this way since she was a child.

So we decided it would be best if I accompanied her from now on. I would act as the cruise director, sex slave, maître d', whatever. I would support Jill so that she could support them. That was our deal.

"You'll see," I told her on the plane, "we're going to have fun this time."

"Just be nice to me," she said. "That'll help a lot."

"Nice to you?"

"Sometimes you get mad at me when I'm around my mother."

"Oh, well . . ." There was some truth in this. She drove me crazy when she was around her mother.

"I don't care," she said. "Just be nice."

Her mom had recently fallen for no apparent reason and Ralph had not been able to pick her up. He had to call 911. This was a problem because they were trying to stay under the radar as far as their health issues were concerned. They thought if the front office found out that they needed assistance, they'd be thrown out of assisted care. I don't know; it's generational, I suppose. I don't think I'll mind getting assistance when I get old. Even now wouldn't be bad.

"We're all headed for suffering and death, baby," I said consolingly. "But that doesn't mean we can't have some laughs along the way. How about we take them out for a great steak tonight?"

"They're both on walkers."

I shrugged. Piece of cake.

Some fifteen years before, we had moved them to Santa Barbara from Madison, Wisconsin, because the cold winters were hard on Lora's arthritis. We were living in Los Angeles at the time and we all agreed that Santa Barbara would be a beautiful place for them to live out their days. And it would be close to us, as well. But not too close, if you know what I mean.

They eventually settled into a lovely retirement community with a beautiful view of the mountains and populated by a large number of retired college professors. This couldn't have been better for Ralph and Lora, who put great stock in intellectual pursuits—Lora, for example, was always sending me books by Noam Chomsky. Their group of friends in Madison had primarily been professors at the University of Wisconsin, so they felt they had found the right crowd.

But then, a couple of years ago, around the time Jill and I moved back to New York, they started to show their age. Ralph had his third heart attack and also suffered from severe, chronic back pain, which could be relieved only by an operation that the doctors refused to give him because of his age. Lora was physically strong, but she was showing a little slippage in the cognizance department. This problem wasn't helped by the fact that she had been seriously hard of hearing since she was in her thirties. She'd been faking conversations for years. A lot of the reason she talked so much was that she couldn't hear anybody else anyway.

In the past four months, Jill had been to Santa Barbara to move them twice: first from their two-bedroom apartment to a smaller one, for financial reasons; and then from independent living to assisted care. The names say it all. Both Ralph and Lora had resisted the move to the assisted-care building, which they dreaded like the Roach Motel: the people check in, but they don't check out. Jill cajoled them into the move by having each one blame it on the other's disabilities. They had gotten to the point where they took great pleasure in each other's failings. Lora virtually beamed when she had to lift things for Ralph, and he delighted in pointing out what she had just forgotten. I really hope we don't get that way. Getting old and sick is hard enough without having to score on each other all the time.

"So, where are you about Italy?" I asked after a long pause. Jill was looking out the window at the Rocky Mountains passing by below us, thinking about her mother, no doubt. Italy was the question of the moment, although neither of us had spoken it aloud. We have a house there that we had bought five years before—a beautiful 350-year-old stone farmhouse amid olive groves in the middle of Umbria; our dream house, our paradise on earth, our new chapter, our life—and now we had a flight booked that would take us there the following week.

"We'll see what the story is when we get to Santa Barbara. But I think maybe we should stick around. Ralph could literally go any day now. He wants to be done with the pain."

"It's a little weird to just sit around and wait for him to die. Like vultures. I think we should go about our lives and then when something happens, we'll respond."

Jill nodded, which meant she heard me but didn't put much stock in what I said. Sometimes she just likes to hear the voice without the content.

We had been putting off going to Italy for over nine months now, which had not been the idea at all. Our original plan was to live there half the year and eventually more. But things kept getting in the way—and not just the trips to see Lora and Ralph. Moving back to New York after almost twenty years in California meant we had to jump-start our theater careers again. All the connections we had from our earlier years in the business were either retired or expired, and the new directors, producers, and casting people had all been too young to stay up and watch *L.A. Law.* We got a lot of blank stares. "Tell us about yourself," they would say. Oy.

We were also busy putting the finishing touches on a documentary film that we'd been working on for almost seven years. It's about an artist friend of ours who just turned ninety years old. He lives on the top of a mountain in Big Sur and he's a big inspiration to us—and to anyone else who meets him. We wanted to get him down on film while he was still around and doing his work. The film kept morphing and re-defining itself, and by the end it was probably the most creative thing either of us had ever been involved with.

Also, I'd just finished doing a play off Broadway, which kept us from going to Italy all through the spring. It was fun, though—dusting off the old acting chops. I played the dad.

So we promised ourselves we would spend the summer—three whole months—in Italy. We'd go in late June and stay through the end of September so that we could catch the grape harvest. Summer is a splendid time to be in Umbria. It's when everybody's *orto* is filled with tomatoes heavy on the vine, basil, arugula, eggplant, and zucchini; it's when everybody's cooking outside—sausages or ribs grilled over a wood fire, washed down with wine we can buy in bulk from a vineyard we know in Montefalco. We bring our jugs and fill them up with a *pistola*—like a gas pump—for two euros a liter.

Summer's when every little village has a *sagra,* which is a festival and feast that a town puts on to raise money for the local *comune*; it always features whatever food the village is best known for, cooked and served by the villagers and their kids. There's the famous onion *sagra* in Canarra, the sausage and celery *sagra* in Trevi, the wild asparagus *sagra* in Eggi—you get the picture.

Summer's also when the big festivals happen. There's the famous Spoleto Festival of Two Worlds, which is mostly classical music and dance; and there's Umbria Jazz in Perugia, which is fast becoming one of Europe's great jazz festivals. Our son Max, who's a drummer, has threatened to come over and visit us this summer so that he can catch Umbria Jazz.

Summer's also when the full cast of characters take the stage. Our wonderful crowd of expats and Italians—some of whom have kids in school or, God forbid, regular jobs, so they can't get away during the year—are all there in the summer and ready for fun. There's this rolling party in our corner of Umbria that opens in early June and plays right through the summer. Sometimes it's a big group gathered around plates of ravioli at the Palazzaccio, our favorite trattoria—actually more like a roadhouse—down on the Via Flaminia. Or it'll be the whole gang over at our place for pizza, baked at 800 degrees Fahrenheit in our wood-burning oven that dates back to the early 1600s; or it could be just Jill and me and another couple at a bar on the piazza in Trevi, talking the night away, spilling secrets like cheap wine. But the party, in whatever size, shape, or configuration, bubbles along like a good, rich soup all summer, and if you're of a mind, all you have to do is slide back the lid and fill your bowl.

Or we could hang around Santa Barbara and wait for Ralph to die.

We know a couple who decided to table their retirement plans until her mother died. The mother was eighty-seven, with inoperable cancer. Twelve years later, when the mother finally kicked off, our friends were too old for anything more strenuous than oatmeal. The idea of this put me into a cold sweat.

And the truth is that Jill would love to go to Italy. She needs it more than I do. She wants it more than I do. Italy is her solace, her refilling station. She's a nature girl, and she's surrounded by it there. She takes walks up the hill to Silvignano, the tiny *borgo* that sits farther up on the mountain above us. Or she'll hike to the top of Poreta—another climb that takes her to a fourteenth-century castle that overlooks the whole Spoleto valley. She loves her breakfasts under the pergola— fresh fruit with yogurt, toast with chestnut honey; maybe I'll make her an omelet from the eggs that Vittoria, our housekeeper and neighbor, brings to us still warm from the hens. Italy is also where Jill takes the time to do her art. Sometimes she'll sit in the shade with her watercolors and paint for hours.

She wants to go to Italy. She's longing for it. But there's no way in the world she can say it. Not while she's writhing in the choke hold of mother-guilt. So she depends on me to twist her arm, because I'm a well-known hedonist who cares about nothing but pleasure. That's our game. She says no; I cajole her into doing it, seemingly against her will; and then we both have a great time. It sounds like a lot of trouble to go through but it's been working for us for years.

# TWO

# Santa Barbara

WE LANDED AT BURBANK AROUND NOON and by the time we got our bags, rented a car, and drove the hour and a half to Santa Barbara, we had blessedly missed lunch at the retirement community. One of my goals for this trip was to avoid eating in the dining room there, although I knew it would be difficult. The arc of my life could be defined by my sidestepping institutional food at any cost, in whatever situation. My military career, for example—or rather the shirking of my military career in the late 1960s—was not about any conscientious or political objection, but more about the fact that I didn't want to eat the food.

We drove straight to Lora and Ralph's apartment and spent the afternoon with them. They were happy to see us, but subdued. They had both been in the hospital in the last few months, and it had sobered them. They seemed smaller to me. They weren't much up for steak that night, so we helped them get some dinner brought to their apartment and sat with them while they picked at it. Then we tucked them in and went off to meet our friends David Rintels and Vicki Riskin, old pals from our days in Los Angeles. They have a beautiful house in Montecito and graciously offered us a place to stay whenever we made these trips. They also provided a sympathetic ear for us—especially for Jill as she tried to put her emotions in some kind of order.

The next morning we hit the ground running. We folded up the walkers, stashed them in the trunk of our car, and set off on a string of errands with Lora and Ralph. And I must say they had quite a bit of energy for a couple of geezers. We went to the pharmacy, the cleaners, and the health food store, and then back to the pharmacy again for everything we forgot. Lora had an appointment with her doctor, which had been scheduled expressly so that Jill could attend and also gave the two of them a chance to have some time alone together. Meanwhile, Ralph and I could do some male bonding, which meant that the moment we were alone he started complaining about Lora.

"You two don't see it. You're not here. But her mind is going. Jill doesn't want to see it."

I tried to cajole him a little bit, reminding him of how many times he repeated the story of his World War II exploits, how often we had charged up Mount Belvedere with him. I urged him to be a little more generous with Lora, to help her rather than criticize. But he just grumbled that we didn't understand, that we didn't want to understand.

"Ask Frankie and Tap! They see it."

Frankie and Tap were good friends of theirs who lived down the hall, whom we had gotten to know pretty well over the years.

"And she can't hear a damn thing. That goddamn hearing aid doesn't work. It *never* worked. We paid thousands for that goddamn thing and all it does is squeal. You can hear the damn thing squealing in the dining room. Everybody's looking around trying to figure out where that damn noise is coming from."

"We're taking her to the hearing aid place on Wednesday and we're going to get that all taken care of," I told him. But this was bullshit because we had been to this place before and there's never anything wrong with the hearing aid. It's a pilot error situation, I'm afraid.

Ralph was in bad shape. His back pain was terrible and he couldn't do anything about it. Well, in some ways he *wouldn't* do anything—he was refusing any kind of medication for pain because he was worried about the side effects. I tried to point out, as diplomatically as I could, that he might not live long enough for the side effects to be an issue, that his problem was right now and the pills would help. But Ralph was the type who believes that pain makes you a better person. Before he retired he was the head of the parole board in Wisconsin. Not a lot of forgiveness there—especially for himself. If I were in his situation, I'd be pounding down those pain pills like Cracker Jacks. Why would anyone want to be in pain? I once had a colonoscopy and the anesthesiologist said to me, "Mr. Tucker, I understand you don't want to feel any pain." I said, "No, you've got it all wrong; I want to feel pleasure." Her eyes lit up and she concocted a cocktail drip for me that was a masterpiece. I remember it as one of the better days I had all year.

So, to say that Ralph and I were from different planets is an understatement. If I had come up before him at the parole board, he would have sent me back to the slammer in a second. Death row. What I am by nature offended him. And vice versa, frankly. But with all that, we actually got along okay; just being male put me on the right side of things, according to his way of thinking—no matter what my other failings were.

He wanted to get me aside to talk about his finances, which he was very concerned about. His daughter, Kathy, had just been to visit with her husband, Chuck, and Ralph had given her a power of attorney. She was now paying all the bills for them, because Ralph didn't feel that Lora was up to it any more. Kathy is a retired college math professor, so she could do all this with ease. She and Chuck lived in Phoenix and they'd been out to visit Lora and Ralph regularly. Jill and Kathy often talked on the phone and compared notes.

Ralph's main agenda was to talk to me about what would be left for Lora after he died. He took all the paperwork out and laid it on the table between us. He knew he had played it wrong with his government pension: it would end with his death, leaving Lora with only Social Security and what they had saved up, which wasn't very much. But he stressed to me that their contract with the retirement community guaranteed that they—or she—could stay in the apartment no matter what. That was their deal. Money or no, Lora would always have this beautiful roof over her head and her community of friends around her.

I could see he was kicking himself about the pension. He had bet against himself. Years back, he figured that with his heart condition and Lora's bout with colon cancer, they wouldn't last that long—so he bet against their longevity and lost. He also showed me all his investment accounts. There wasn't much; a few mutual funds and some bonds. He had lost some money with Enron in one account, and this infuriated him. He railed on about those "greedy bastards," and I frankly enjoyed listening. The angrier he got, the younger and stronger he seemed. He clearly thrived on anger, which is one way to get to ninety-one, I suppose.

I told him that he didn't have to worry about Lora—at least in terms of money; that we would be there as a safety net for whatever she needed. And then he started to cry. Not, I thought, for himself; he wasn't mawkish that way. But maybe for all the things he could have done and didn't, or for all the things he did do and shouldn't have done. I think life had seemed so painfully long for him recently, and now it seemed short. He talked again about his years in the army. Here we go again up Mount Belvedere. He had been in the infantry in Italy and he saw a lot of action; he saw friends die. It was the defining part of his life.

When Jill and Lora came back from the doctor, we left them to rest up and we drove over to the Rintelses' house to take a nap ourselves. On the way, Jill caught me up on her mom's situation. The doctor—a woman whom Jill was very high on—was concerned about Lora's falling. It seemed she was blacking out and they hadn't been able to figure out why, but the doctor was ordering more tests. She was also concerned about Lora's emotional state.

"She's scared," said Jill. "She's really panicked that he's going to die."

"Well, he will."

"And it's making her paranoid."

"Like what?"

"I don't know—all kinds of crazy stuff." She got a funny look on her face.

"What?"

"Well, first of all, she's convinced that Ralph is talking about her behind her back. She thinks he's telling all their friends that she's losing it."

"He is. He was just railing to me about it. That's not paranoia."

"Well, . . . there's more."

"What?"

"There's this guy. He drives the van for the retirement community but Ralph hires him on the side to drive him to all his doctor's appointments and wherever else he has to go."

"So?"

"Well, he doesn't share him with my mom. He won't let her use him. She has to find her own way to get to the drug-store and everything."

"Why won't he share him?"

"I don't know. It's hard to tell because my mom is so weird about it."

She made a face like, *Look, don't blame me; I'm just the messenger here; I didn't write this shit.*

"What?"

"Well . . ." She shook her head again. "She's very paranoid about the two of them."

"What do you mean?"

"About what they're doing when they're out all that time."

"Why? What are they doing? You mean she thinks they're getting it on? In the van?"

Jill shrugged.

"Honey, Jesus Christ!"

"I know."

"He's ninety-one years old! He can't even get his pants off by himself."

"I know."

"She really thinks Ralph is gay? After all these years?"

"She gets weird. She has all kinds of paranoid things going on. Remember when she thought we were laundering money in the Cayman Islands?"

"Yeah, but this is a little far-fetched even for your mother. I mean we were actually in the Cayman Islands and people are known to launder money there, so, you know, there's at least some kind of reason for her mind to go there, but this is . . ."

"Well," said Jill after a neatly timed pause, "he does wear those white shoes sometimes."

# THREE

# Alison

LATER THAT AFTERNOON WE WENT BACK to Ralph and Lora's for an early dinner. They had reserved a big table in the main dining room so that we could spend an evening with their friends, many of whom we'd gotten to know over the years. Since they moved to the assisted-care building, they were expected to eat in the smaller dining room there, which was, frankly, a pretty depressing affair. But the rules allowed them to go back and eat with their unassisted friends whenever they got a table together.

Also joining us was our daughter, Alison, who drove up from Los Angeles to spend an evening with her grandparents—and to see her parents, of whom she is very fond. The idea was to do the early dinner with Ralph and Lora and their friends, bundle them all off to bed, and then the three of us would go out to get some Mexican food.

Alison is my daughter from my first marriage, and therein lies a tale. Jill and I met around the time of Alison's first birthday—so that makes it the fall of 1970. Eight months or so later I left my wife and moved in with Jill. A few weeks after that (after much intense discussion, as you can imagine, between the three adults), Alison came to live with Jill and me, and for all practical purposes she has been with us ever since. She's always continued to see her natural mom and has a full-on relationship with her but Jill has been her de facto mother since around the time she started to walk and talk. And Ralph and Lora were her de facto grandparents for all that time—along with Jill's father and *his* second wife. Then on my side of the family, of course, there were my parents, who had stayed married to each other for their whole miserable lives.

But defacto isn't blood. And Alison, who is quite savvy and—yes, a little dramatic—has always been sensitive to the difference, both with Jill and with the grandparents on Jill's side. And her drama became all the more biblical when she was around age twelve and our son Max was born. Somehow, stupidly, we didn't see the storm looming. When we learned that Jill was pregnant we went right to Alison to break the news.

"How would you feel about having a little baby brother or sister?" we asked with barely concealed excitement. She had been talking about wanting this for a long time.

"I'd *hate* it! *Don't do it!*" She said, and stomped out of the room.

Oh dear, we thought, too late for that. And thus began nine months of the silent treatment, tears, shouting, and tons and tons of dead baby jokes. After Max was born and she was able to put a face to her fears, she lightened up a little, but their life as siblings got off to a dodgy start to say the least.

The relationship between Jill and Alison—the stepmom syndrome—has been complicated, obviously. They've had over thirty-five years to work on it and I would say it's at least as good as most other mother-daughter pair ups I've seen. But there was a moment in their history—a crucible—that woke them both up to how much they meant to each other. A year after Max was born, Alison went off for a vacation with Biological Mom, as she did every year. This was a special trip that included Alison's British grandfather. It was to be a merry jaunt by horse-drawn caravan around the Dingle peninsula in Ireland. Halfway through the trip I got a call in New York that Alison had been hit by a car, was hospitalized, and was in a coma. Jill and I bundled up the baby and flew off to Ireland, not knowing in what condition we would find her when we got there.

We spent the better part of a month alternating twelve-hour shifts at the hospital, first waiting for her to come out of the coma and then waiting to see how much damage had been done to her brain and her body. We sat and watched her face and waited for her personality, her essence, to reappear. It was during this month that Jill came to realize she was and would always be the mother of this child. It took a full year for the head injuries to heal and Alison still has pain in her hip when it rains, but she's whole and healthy now.


Alison is a chef, a very talented one. She does catering and private dinners because she doesn't like the pressure of restaurant cooking. And yes, I take a lot of fatherly pride in the fact that she's so good at what she does and that she chose a profession so close to my own aspirations; I would have been a chef for sure if I hadn't gone into acting. Alison started out her professional life in the family business, going to drama school in New York and then going to Los Angeles to give acting a shot. She did pretty well for a while, but she wasn't cut out for the rejection part. I'll tell you, I wasn't cut out for it either—for her rejections, I mean, not mine. I've been rejected so many times I kind of miss it when it doesn't happen; but with your kid it's hard.

Then one day she decided she'd had enough of show biz and enrolled herself in a culinary school. She got her license and started working as a sous chef with various caterers. Then she threw weekly dinner parties at her house, which started with friends and then friends of friends, and the circle expanded, as did her reputation. She started booking jobs and it grew into a nice little business. As I said, she's very good.

We teamed up with Alison that evening at around 5:30 at Ralph and Lora's apartment. After looking through some albums of pictures of Alison as a toddler that Lora had put together, we rounded up the walkers and made our way down to the main dining room. Alison sat between Ralph and Lora so that they could take full advantage of having a granddaughter to show off. They've been good grandparents to her through the years, although she and Ralph have had their moments; Alison's rebellious teenage years coincided with Ralph's Scotch-drinking years, and there were some rough exchanges. Alison thought she had to defend Lora from Ralph's harsh criticism, and Ralph needed to point out Alison's disrespect for her elders. They were both quite right. But then as the years passed, Ralph stopped drinking, Alison grew up, and they learned to tolerate each other.

There has always been a kind of sisterhood between Lora and Alison. They're both iconoclasts: they both love to be the unique person in the room, and they recognize and respect these traits in each other. Lora has been shocking her family for longer than she remembers. She was the youngest of six in a Church of the Brethren clan in Ohio and she's the only one who ever really got out of town. She met Jill's dad, Dale Eikenberry, at the Brethren's college and got to know Dale's father, who was a distinguished professor of psychology. The father introduced her to the life of the intellect and she was changed forever. The proudest thing she could ever say about herself was that she was "intellectually curious."

Dale enlisted in the navy a few days after Pearl Harbor, and during his time at officer candidate school he rushed home to Ohio and married Lora. Then he was shipped off to the front. Lora passed the war years teaching school and working at various "Rosie the Riveter" jobs until Dale came home. Then they went to Yale, where he studied law under the GI Bill. They lived romantically in a Quonset hut on the Yale campus; they hung out with the Yalies; they took trips to Cuba for fun. And Jill thinks it was sometime during the Yale years that they left the Church of the Brethren and became Unitarians. Lora was always a caution.

The talk at the table that night was totally enjoyable. This was an educated, liberal-leaning crowd and the conversation swung from politics to the economy to health care for the elderly (of course) to poetry and finally to the current baseball season. At one point Lora held forth eloquently about the wetlands in Wisconsin and the need to preserve them in the face of encroaching real estate development. It was all very impressive.

Of course there wasn't an older person at the table who didn't have some serious health condition. The friends didn't spend the evening talking about their problems, but Ralph and Lora had given us a rundown before we came down to dinner. Across from me were Parkinson's and the early stages of Alzheimer's; to their right were kidney prob-

lems and throat cancer, in remission; to my right were Mr.
and Mrs. Diabetes—two different types. There wasn't a person at the table who wasn't looking the Reaper full in the face,
but you wouldn't have known it from the conversation.

I artfully pushed my food around my plate, hiding some
of it under the iceberg lettuce, but none of it actually passed
my lips. Mrs. Diabetes to my right noticed and tried to get
me to eat something.

"Try the turkey drumettes. They're my favorite."

I nodded and said, "Mmmm" with as much enthusiasm as I
could muster. But there's no way I was going to eat any of that
crap. What is a turkey drumette, anyway? Think about it. What
part of the body?

Later, Jill, Alison, and I were sipping margaritas at a nice
Mexican place in Montecito—well, Jill was carefully nursing
her glass of white wine—and we were talking about Alison's
move to New York, which was coming up soon. She'd decided
to make the move when she was in New York for Jill's sixtieth
birthday party a few months before. Alison grew up in New
York, went through college there, and, like us, felt more at
home there than in Los Angeles. She said she was moving because it was time to change her life around, maybe lose some
toxic relationships and rekindle some old good ones: she had
gotten married in Los Angeles back in the early nineties and
divorced a year later. I think she was ready to leave that behind. She said she missed the seasons changing. But I think she
missed us. Max lives in New York, and once Jill and I moved
back, Alison felt left out of the family. We thought it was a
great idea. Her plan was to rent her house in Los Angeles and
find an apartment for about the same money. Then she'd start
establishing her catering business again. We had all kinds
of plans to help her, including inviting rich friends over for

dinner—people who could use a personal chef sometimes—and having Alison do the meal. Then we'd hand out her cards. Slam dunk.

"When do you leave for Italy?" asked Alison, scooping some salsa onto the end of a chip.

"Eight days," I answered.

"If we go," added Jill.

Alison shot one of her looks: is Mom going into martyr mode?

"I just think I'll be nervous the whole time. I don't know if I can have any fun. Ralph is talking about dying every day. He really is ready to go."

"Well, he'll die when he dies; there's nothing you can do about it."

"I could help my mom."

I just sat there, sipped my drink, and kept my mouth shut. Alison was carrying my silks.

"Look," said Alison, making a gesture with her hands that says *Here's the whole thing in a nutshell.* "When you and dad get old, do you expect me to give up my whole life, put on a nurse's uniform, and hover around you, waiting for you to drop?"

"Of course not."

"Well, neither does your mother."

Jill gave a deep sigh. Her whole life was in that sigh. Then she nodded.

"Whew!" said Alison, "For a minute there I thought you were gonna say, 'Yes, come and take care of me when I get old; change my diapers; wipe my chin.' Whoa, I need another margarita."

We laughed and then Jill asked, "Did I tell you what my shrink said?"

"I didn't even know you were seeing somebody."

"Yeah, I started a couple of months ago. It's been amazing. I didn't tell you?"

"Maybe you did. You're always doing some kind of therapy, aren't you?"

Jill let that pass.

"So what did he tell you?"

"She. Martha. She's . . . besides being a full-blown Jungian therapist, she's . . . an intuitive—a shaman, actually."

Alison took that in stride; she's seen us go through any number of New Age type things when we lived in northern California.

"So what did she say?"

"She told me she had a dream where my mother was underwater and I was on the surface, and she was pulling me down. She told me that my mother didn't want to die without me."

"Jesus."

"Yeah," I added. ""When I heard that, a serious chill went up my spine."

"What did she think you should do about it?" asked Alison.

Jill shrugged. "An exorcism, maybe."

"Wow. You guys."

I looked at Jill; she gave me a tired smile. It didn't matter what her shrink said, what I said, what Alison said; Jill was going to worry about her mom. When she was fifteen years old, her beloved dad walked out on them for another woman and Lora fell apart. She lay down on the bedroom floor and started to cry and Jill didn't know if she would ever stop. After that, Lora started referring to Jill as her "rock," which is what she became. It wasn't until recently—with this current therapist—that Jill allowed herself to get to any of her own emotions about her father's sudden departure.

When I first met Lora she kept her distance from me. After all, I was a married man who had abandoned his wife and child to have an affair with her daughter. Talk about touching a nerve. And I had just as much of a problem warming up to her. She didn't get my jokes, for one thing. Later, I realized that she couldn't hear them, but it was still disconcerting to get those blank stares all the time. It really wasn't so much that I didn't like Lora; it was more that I didn't like Jill when she was around Lora. She became a different woman—guilt-ridden, apprehensive, and doting. I didn't like this woman; I wanted Jill back. It took me a lot of years to realize that there was no other woman; it's just another part of Jill. And if I'm going to love her, I have to love all of her. A woman isn't a chicken; you can't buy parts.

Alison asked me to get the check. She still had to drive back to Los Angeles.

"The only thing that counts is that the two of us are on the same side," I said to Jill. "Otherwise we're lost."

She nodded and took my hand.

"Let's go to Italy," she said.

# FOUR

# Elmview

THE NEXT MORNING, WE HAD COFFEE with a Buddhist nun. I'll explain. We had to find a replacement for our friend Alix, who had been helping out with Ralph and Lora over the last few years. Alix had been the caretaker of the house we owned in Big Sur during our television days. She also did all our bookkeeping. Her son, Talon, is our godson, whatever that means. I suppose if I don't know, I'm not a very good godparent.

After we sold the Big Sur house out from under them, Alix and Talon moved down to the Santa Ynez area, just over the mountain from Santa Barbara. So, in addition to being our bookkeeper, she hired on in the role of substitute daughter for Lora and Ralph. This job entailed dropping in on them a couple of times a week, taking them to their doctors' appointments (she took comprehensive notes each time so that she could explain everything to them—and to Jill—afterward), making sure they got all their prescriptions, running errands, and having the occasional lunch with Lora for the requisite girl talk.

But Alix's life was changing. She had met a guy—Jake—and things were getting serious between them. Beside their courtship, Alix was working for Jake, managing his life and business as she had so brilliantly managed ours over the years. But that meant she had to give up some of the time she spent with Lora and Ralph. She would continue to take them to their doctors' appointments, but she had to give up squiring them around town for anything else.

This didn't affect Ralph as much, because he had his van driver to take him around—and the less said about that, the better—but Jill wanted someone to help Lora. Enter the Buddhist nun. We got her name through Vicki Rintels, our hostess in Montecito. Vicki is a big-time Buddhist who works with worldwide organizations like the Tibetan Aid Foundation and she has close ties to the Buddhist community in Santa Barbara. She thought this particular nun, who had done a lot of work in elder care, would be perfect for the job.

We met at her house in a modest section of Santa Barbara and Jill, who meditates on a daily basis, went for her immediately. I had reservations. Yes, she was calm and patient and had a lovely sense of humor, but when we described what her duties would be she brought up a small problem.

"You do know that I don't have car?" she asked quietly.

"No car?"

"No. I don't drive."

"How do you get around?"

"Public transportation. It's quite easy."

"Well, you know," I said, "Lora's on a walker."

"Yes. That would be no problem."

We talked about a few other details and then told her we'd let her know in a couple of days. I thought it was odd to hire a nondriver for the job of driving someone around town, but I was outvoted.

"She's great," said Jill, beaming. "There's something about the idea of my mom hanging out with a Buddhist nun that's really appealing to me. It's perfect. It makes me feel better about going away."

Case closed.

When we arrived at Ralph and Lora's building, Josie, who ran the assisted care program, headed us off and asked if we could come into her office for a moment. After some quick chitchat, she ominously closed the door.

"I had a meeting with Ralph last week."

"Yeah," I said. "He was telling me about it. About the contract they have with you and that . . ."

"About a lot of things, actually."

Pause, pause.

Jill's antennae shot up.

"What?"

Another pause.

"I want to talk to you about Elmview," said Josie in a tone that was slightly overripe, just a little too friendly, like when the doctor wants to speak with you privately in his office.

Elmview is the dementia ward. Well, it's not a ward; it's quite nice, actually. Josie walked us over and gave us a tour. It has individual studio apartments and a center area where everybody gathers. It also has access to the outside, and there's a garden. It's airy and nice and filled with people who basically don't know where or who they are. They were watching a  video about exercise for the elderly on television, and a few were trying to follow it, but most of them were staring off.

Jill, at this point, was rigid with tension. "My mother is not ready for this yet, Josie. Not even close."

"I know that, Jill. Believe me, I do. But I wanted you to see what's going on here, because it's really a wonderful place."

"Oh, I'm sure . . ."

"No, not just for the patients, but just to be in here; can't you feel it?"

We stood for a moment, pretending to feel it. At least I did. Jill was probably feeling it.

"They've let go—of putting up a false front, of struggling to be what they're not any more. There's something wonderful about that."

This got Jill—because she was always talking about how exhausting it must be to be her mom. Lora's been pretending to hear for fifty years; now she's pretending to remember.

"I don't think your mom belongs here now, Jill. But Ralph thinks . . . after he passes on . . ."

"Ralph is exaggerating, Josie. He does this. I don't know why; maybe it takes his mind off dying or something, but he . . . he undermines her; he puts pressure on her to remember things, and because of the pressure, she can't. And he's very charming in public and everyone thinks he's just the greatest, but he . . . he's undermining her."

"Jill . . ."

"No, it's fine. Thank you for showing us this place. It really is wonderful and I'm sure when she's ready for it my mom will love it, too. So thanks. Really."

"I want to have a lunch here—tomorrow—with the four of you. Okay? Ralph, Lora, and the two of you."

She was pushing it. Jill took a breath.

"Sure, that would be great."

"I think we should tell Lora that we'd love to have her help out here; because we know that she's done some social work in the past, hasn't she?"

Jill nodded.

"I'll call them right now and set it up, okay?"

"Fine," said Jill.

"Fine" is a word Jill uses when she means it's not fine at all. She was steaming.

"That bastard," she said as we walked away. "He's gaslighting her. And he's lining everybody up against her."

The gaslight reference was to the old movie of that name. Jill had her mom cast in Ingrid Bergman's role and Ralph was Charles Boyer's evil character. In the movie, Charles slowly, insidiously drives Ingrid out of her mind by turning the gaslights up and down. This is a theme that Jill has been harping on for years, long before her mom and Ralph became old and infirm—that Ralph's strictness, his perfectionism, put Lora on the defensive so she couldn't be her real, creative, multi-directional, somewhat bubbleheaded self. In short, he wanted her to think the way he did and when she couldn't—or chose not to—he made the case that something was wrong with her and needed to be fixed. Lora, as a defense, poked fun at his seriousness; this, of course, enraged him. That was the game they played. But now, with time running out in the fourth quarter, the game was getting grim.

That evening we had plans to take Ralph and Lora to a Chinese place they liked for an early dinner. Alix and her boyfriend, Jake, would join us. But at the last minute, Ralph bailed out, saying he didn't feel up to it. He tried to encourage Lora to go on her own, but she opted to stay home with him.

At dinner Jill wanted Alix's take on everything that was happening. Alix was in a tough position. She was the hub. Lora used her as a confidante to complain about Ralph's verbal abuse; Ralph took her aside to complain about Lora's loss of memory and frequent flights of paranoia. When Kathy, Ralph's daughter, was visiting, she took her dad's side, of course, and tried to persuade Alix to support his interpretation of the drama. And now Alix had to deal with Jill, who, besides being her friend of fifteen years, was also her employer. Touchy, touchy position to be in, and I watched Alix tightrope her way through it.

"You know, your mom is fine most of the time. We had lunch last week and talked for hours and she didn't miss a beat. And then there are times when she forgets stuff. Gosh, I hope I'm that sharp when I'm eighty-seven!"

"I hate to say it, but I think she's going to be much better after Ralph goes," said Jill, looking for support on this theory. "He makes her panic and that's the worst thing for someone who's trying to remember."

"Well, you know, he's in pain and that's so hard to live with. I think he really loves her."

"I know he does. He really does. But . . . she doesn't have those problems when she's just with me. I mean . . . she forgets things sometimes . . . but so does Mike, for God's sake."

I waved across the table and thanked her for pointing that out.

Lunch the next day at Elmview was a lovely affair. There were some children from a local school who came to sing for the old folks and do crafts with them. Then the staff grilled hot dogs and hamburgers and we all had a picnic outside in the sunshine. It was the best meal I had on the grounds all week. Afterward, Lora and Ralph sat and visited with a couple of friends of theirs—both widowed—who had recently been moved to Elmview. Lora was impressive—definitely on her game in this situation. She had brought some photos of a big dinner they had all been to together a year before, and she sat with them for a long time, pointing out the different people in the photos and naming them, over and over. She had patience, empathy, and not a drop of condescension, plus some real knowledge of how to deal with people who had dementia. Jill took pains to make sure that Josie caught the whole scene. It looked as if she was trying to prove something to herself as much as to Josie.

The next morning we went over to say good-bye. Both Ralph and Lora were in a pretty chipper frame of mind, probably trying to make it easier on us. When I shook Ralph's hand and then gave him a very masculine little hug, I wondered if this was to be the last time I would ever see him. But then I remembered I had thought that a few times before. Lora and Jill were chatting away about some people they knew in Madison, Wisconsin—the Lardys—about how they were still kayaking in the lake in their eighties and about how Hank still went to the lab every day. That was the way Lora was—always talking about something or someone else rather than just being there with you, in the moment that you're actually in. Jill once told me that her greatest wish was to be able to just sit with her mom in some lovely place, in silence, and hold hands.

Finally, Jill hugged her and said that she would call her every day from Italy. Lora smiled her ironic smile and patted Jill's arm.

# FIVE

# Alitalia

I WON'T LIE AND SAY THAT MY HEART DIDN'T LEAP with joy when the wheels went up on our transatlantic flight and the bar cart started its merry way up the aisle. Jill and I sat quietly, each with our own thoughts, which is pretty standard for us when our plane is taking off. It's a good time to take stock of things—that moment before you either soar into space on an exciting journey or crash in a fiery ball at the end of the runway.

I was thinking we were doing pretty well, the two of us. We managed to get on the same side of the problem even though our viewpoints were different. My view was basically philosophical—that we're all going to die in the end and our task is to live well until that happens—while Jill's was purely emotional: she wanted to save her mom and she was the only person in the world who could do it. Okay, there's no reason these two views can't live together. All we have to do is find a way to fold Jill's mission into our good time in Italy. Eminently doable. We could have dinner parties, for example, and invite only people whose parents were old and failing—easily done in our crowd—or we could set aside a special time every day for Jill's phone call to her mom and I could let it happen without drop-ping sarcastic comments. Yep, that would be a good one.

After we hit cruising altitude, Jill turned to me and squeezed my hand. She looked great. Her eyes were clear, like they are after she meditates; her smile was real and loving—not the false smile she puts on sometimes to make me feel better. This is good, I thought; we did the right thing. The stew-ardess came by to tell us what was for dinner, but I passed. No airplane food; two glasses of red wine, half an Ambien, and good night, Irene.

Alessandra greeted us the next morning at Fiumicino, Rome's main airport. We had first met her a couple of years before when we rented a film at her video store in Spoleto. She's an enterprising young mom who augments her earnings at the store by offering a taxi service to and from the Rome airports. As we emerged from customs we saw her jumping up and down and waving to us emotionally, as if we were her long-lost relatives coming home from the war. We all hugged, and the two girls started jabbering furiously in Italian, "How's your son? How's your mom? Tell me everything"—etcetera. When they finally settled down, Alessandra turned to me.

"*Un caffè, sì?*"

"*Sì, certo,*" I replied, and we all schlepped the luggage down to the end of the arrivals area, where there's a bar. This is a tradition with us; before we get into the car to drive home, I get to taste my first cup of Italian espresso at the airport bar. A bar in Italy is very different from its counterpart in the states. It's more a daytime thing, with coffee, sweet rolls, and sandwiches. Yes, there's some booze on the shelves—in case any customers want a *digestivo* after lunch or a shot of grappa in their coffee (which is called *caffè corretto,* "corrected coffee") —but Italian bars are more brightly lit, family kinds of places.

Jill has her tradition at the bar as well. While I'm having my espresso she orders a sandwich—usually some kind of ham or salami with cheese, lettuce, and tomato. It's a symbolic act because she eats it with the bread and all—like a proper sandwich, rather than picking all the protein out as she does in the states. Jill has completely different eating habits when she's in Italy. It's like another person lurks inside her and emerges just after we collect our luggage. In New York, her digestion is very delicate; she can't eat garlic, onions, beans, or anything related to the cabbage family; she rarely touches bread, rice, or pasta; she eats no sweets. In Italy, the other person—the Italian lurker—eats all these things with gusto and never has a moment's trouble with them.

We jabbered away the whole trip to Umbria, switching from our fractured Italian to Alessandra's fractured English and back again. Her son had been born with some serious physical and mental challenges and she caught us up on his progress with the doctors. Jill brought her up-to-date on the details of Lora's situation, which Alessandra knew Jill was worried about from our last visit, nine months before. The conversation was personal, even intimate—like a talk you would have with a close family member. And she's just the woman we rent videos from.

Our one stop before reaching home was at Laura's *pasta fresca* store, which is about a mile down the road from our house. Yes, *pasta fresca* means fresh, homemade egg pasta—fettuccini, tortellini, ravioli stuffed with various treasures—and you can't get better, more succulent, more fresh-egg-flavorful pasta than at Laura's store. But we were there for another reason. Domenico, Laura's husband, is our gardener and caretaker, and he stores our car in his garage when we're away. So we needed to stop by and pick it up on our way home. We got there around 12:30, just before lunch, and there were still a few customers in the store. We thought we would wait quietly until everyone was served, but Laura spied us from the kitchen.

"*Bentornati! Bentornati!*" That means, literally, "well-returned"—a great way of saying it. Laura pulled us back into the kitchen, which is also where the family hangs out, and launched a barrage of Italian that I missed most of. My ear wasn't quite attuned properly yet. But the gist of it was something about how their daughter had seen Jill in a television movie and no one believed it when she told her class about it. Or she said that her daughter had just flown to Argentina with Jill to open a dress shop. I'm not sure. Laura speaks an Umbrian dialect that's not always so easy to understand. But I nodded and said things that would be appropriate responses to either story.

Domenico came in and we did the whole "*Bentornati*" moment again and he told me that our car was already at the house waiting for us. But before we could get out the door, Laura made a care package for us: some tortellini stuffed with veal, cheese, and mortadella and a pound or so of fettuccini, just in case. Then she dug in the fridge and found a meat sauce—sort of an Umbrian version of a Bolognese that was stored in an Umbrian version of Tupperware, and she put that on top of the pile. Then she put in a raspberry *torta*—Laura also specializes in desserts. And she wouldn't let us pay for anything; she never does. Clearly we're overpaying Domenico.

Then Laura took Jill aside and held her arm tightly, "*Come stá la mamma?*" How's your mom. Everyone in the neighborhood knows that Jill is worried about her mom; this qualifies her for sainthood in Italy.

Laura is the hardest-working person I have ever known. Her energy is astonishing. Early in the morning—every morning—she makes the pasta and sends her kids off to school; then she runs the store, cleans the house upstairs, cooks dinner, does the dishes, and probably snuggles up to her husband, all in one day, every day. On Monday when the store is closed, she caters private parties. But this energy also drives the biggest heart in central Umbria. She's generous with everything—her humor, her husband, her opinions, her ravioli. She has this wonderful laugh, a throaty kind of chortle that peppers its way through everything she says. It can mean almost anything, depending on the accompanying hand gestures and eyebrow raisings.

"Believe me (heh, heh), it's not so easy to grow old (heh, heh, heh)."

With this she holds out the thumb and little finger of her right hand and rocks it back and forth, while tilting her head and lifting her eyebrows all the way up into her hairline. Try it sometime; it's very effective. I love talking to Laura, even if I rarely know what's she's saying.


Our house, known locally as the Rustico, sits in a perfect spot—perfect for us, at least. For thirty-five years, whenever we were looking for a house we told the real estate agent that we wanted something high up with a dramatic view, and every time we ended up with a house that was tucked into the side of the hill in a protected way. The Rustico is tucked in. It's only a bit of the way up the hill, with a calmer, more benign view of the valley; but having the mountain behind comforts us, I think. The mountain watches our back.

The house was all spiffed up to welcome us when we arrived—thanks to Vittoria, who takes care of it as if it were her own. She made sure that all the bugs, mice, and scorpions who were house-sitting for us had been shooed away. She opened the shutters and let the summer breeze blow through the white linen curtains in our bedroom. Fresh coffee, sugar, and some *cornetti*—the Italian version of croissants, usually stuffed with jelly—were sitting on the kitchen table waiting for us, alongside a bowl of fresh eggs from Vittoria's chickens. Vittoria is Domenico's aunt, and she lives a few miles farther up the mountain. She was born and bred in the neighborhood, but she spent her working years in the employ of the Agnelli family, of Fiat fame. So she's traveled the world in very sophisticated circles for most of her life. But when she decided to retire, she came back home. She only cares for our house because she loves it and remembers it from when she was a little girl. And because we live there, she takes care of us as well.

After I wrestled the luggage inside, we walked around and remembered things. The house seemed bigger to me this time. Sometimes it's bigger than I remember, sometimes smaller. This must have something to do with expectations.

I walked out the kitchen door and over to the pergola that shelters our outdoor dining table. It seats twelve people comfortably and we've had up to twenty-two, quite uncomfortably, crowding in for a pizza party. The wood-burning grill, which is my new prized possession, sits close by—against the side wall of the oven. It's a backyard version of a *sagra* grill, which is used to feed hundreds of people at a time. The logs burn in an iron basket at the back of the grill and as the coals drop down you pull them forward as you need them with a rake like a croupier's. So it's a continuous-feed situation; just keep the basket full of logs and you can grill all night.

The wood-burning oven, the *forno a legna,* has been standing there long before there was a house. It was the neighborhood oven in the early 1600s. The early 1600s—and we're still cooking in it.

Jill was upstairs, unpacking the suitcases and playing house, rearranging the storage space so that she had room for all her things, neatly arranged in the two closets and the eight ample drawers of the dresser. I would be allotted a small, narrow shelf in the bottom of one of the closets.

We were jet-lagged but we knew we should wait to crash until after dinner, so we drove into town to get some staples to stock the pantry. I took the scenic route, through the little town of Poreta, whose main drag is so narrow only one car can scrape through at a time. And there's usually an old dog who takes his afternoon nap in the middle of the road and he's too deaf and bored to respond to a horn. Sometimes you just have to sit there and wait until his mood changes. When you clear the few ancient houses—and the dog—the road opens up into fields of wheat, sunflowers, tobacco, and, in the spring, red poppies all the way to the horizon.

I had e-mailed all our Umbrian friends to see who would be available to meet us at the Palazzaccio that night for dinner. It's my way of assuring myself a warm welcome. The Palazzaccio—full name: Trattoria Tipica al Palazzaccio, "da Piero"—is our hangout. We're good friends with the family who own it, and they serve the most honest meal on earth. It's an Italian truck stop, really. Piero was a trucker and his wife cooked for him and his friends; that's how it started. Piero's gone now, but mamma's still around and the daughters, Danila, Teresa, and Nicla, the "Three Sisters of Umbria," run the place. What you get there is simple, fresh, plentiful homemade food served in a family setting by generous people —that's all they have.

After the pasta course and the *secondi* were packed away—
for me that was *castrato* (grilled lamb chops, olive oil, salt, and
pepper)—and before the dessert and grappa, Jill sneaked out
to the parking lot to call her mom on her *telefonino*. This pro-
voked a long and, ultimately, grappa-fueled conversation
about our parents and our obligations; about how different it
was in Italy, where the families stay a lot closer together. Then
the conversation veered to our own impending old age and
about how we would react when some son or daughter sat us
down to talk about taking our car keys away because we were
too old and feeble to be behind the wheel.

Danila came by to clear the table and offer more grappa,
which is served out of a big green glass jug that never seems
to empty.

"Danila," called Bruno, who was born in Rome and whose
mom lives on her own down there and refuses to move out of
her house, "*Che ci fai con tua mamma?*" What are you doing with
your mother?

"*Sta in cucina,*" said Danila with a grin. "*Facendo i ravioli.*"
We put her in the kitchen, she said, making ravioli until she
drops.

# SIX

# Settling In

I WAS UP AT DAWN. It's all well and good to say you'll stay awake the whole day after you fly so that you'll turn yourself around and beat the jet lag, but I think that's just for young people. I would have been better off with a nap. And the grappa, which seemed like a great idea the night before, turned itself into sugar around four in the morning; my eyes popped open and that was it. Never drink on the day you fly. It's a dehydration thing. I should remember that.

Jill was blissfully dreaming away, so I tiptoed over to the open French doors and took in the sounds and sights of the morning. Our bedroom's on the second floor and we have a great view down into the valley. The mountain behind us keeps the house in shade until around eight or so, but the Spoleto valley in the middle distance, with its wide swaths of farmland, olive groves, and vineyards, was already warming itself in the morning sun; beyond it the mountains that lead to Todi and Orvieto were gray-blue, as they always are. It doesn't matter if the sun is directly on them or if it's setting behind them in the evening; they always have the same smoky blue color that frames the silver and green of the olive trees.

The birds were all up, too, having their breakfast and chattering away. There are some swallows—*rondini*—that like to hang around our pool. Maybe they think it's a good place to pick up chicks. They were flying in a big circle—a lot like the landing pattern at La Guardia—up over the house, then around to the hill of olive trees on the right of us, then out toward the valley, where they banked into a wide turn and then headed directly back at me. When they got to the pool, just below me, they swooped down, each one in turn—maybe ten seconds apart—and dive-bombed the surface, leaving just the tiniest ripples, before they climbed steeply over the house and circled around again. I couldn't tell whether they were taking sips of water or scooping up some tiny bugs on the surface, but I watched their show until the sun crested our mountain and lit the house, the pool, the birds, and me in fresh sunlight.

I didn't hear Jill slip out of bed. She tiptoed up from behind and put her arms around me; her body, still cozy from bed, felt warm against my back. We just stood there in the breeze that blows up from the valley and watched the birds. This is what we came for, I thought. To be transported. And by that I don't mean just getting away from our problems or changing the scenery, but actually stepping outside ourselves to get a whiff of the whole thing, the whole fabric of life, death, and renewal.

At breakfast we made a long list of everything we needed to stock the house. Then we were off—to the supermarket first for things like toilet paper and washing machine detergent; then to a vineyard in Montefalco to lay in some good, neighborhood wine that goes down so well with the local produce;

then to the *tartufi* man down the road for a few fresh summer truffles—to grate over eggs in the morning or to slice razor-thin for putting under the skin of a roasting chicken. And leaving the best for last, we went to Ugo, our *macellaio,* our butcher, our friend.

Ugo's shop is on the edge of our little town. There are usually two or three people waiting patiently in line. You have to be patient at Ugo's—especially if you're buying his famous house-made prosciutto, which he slices carefully by hand. People—aficionados of great prosciutto—come from as far as Rome to watch him do his thing. First he puts an edge on his knife, which is a long, thin blade that was surely used by his father and grandfather before him. Then he trims the prosciutto, taking off some of the dark, outer rind and the extraneous fat, so that his slices are perfect. He starts from the far end and saws carefully toward his body, like a master cellist bowing away. The delicate scallop of dark-pink ham curls over the knife as he slices, and when he gets to the end, he picks up a pair of small metal tongs and lifts the treasure delicately off the ham and lays it on the waiting butcher paper. Then he starts the next piece. Don't go to Ugo for prosciutto if you're in a hurry to get back home to watch the ball game.

When we entered his store through the fly curtain, which is made of strips of hanging material that let in the breeze but keep out the flies, Ugo smiled and waved.

"*Benarrivati!*" That's another way to say "welcome home" in Italian. He came from behind the counter, interrupting his attention to another customer, to give us each a hug and a kiss on both cheeks. Then we waited our turn, reading the soccer scores in the local paper that Ugo always has available.

We ordered some prosciutto first. Twenty minutes later, he had sliced about 150 grams, which is a little over a quarter pound. We got some pork sausages to have on hand and then had him wrap up a nice *guanciale* that was hanging on a hook behind the counter. Guanciale is the cheek of the pig that's been slowly cured with salt and pepper in Ugo's back room. It's a kind of bacon, fatter and more flavorful than pancetta and not smoked like American bacon. It's great for using in pasta sauces—especially *amatriciana* or carbonara. But that day, Ugo had another recipe for us. I'll translate:

"For a nice salad, sauté some *guanciale,* cut up into bite-size pieces, in a pan until the fat gets rendered out—don't add any oil! Then sizzle in some vinegar and fresh, chopped sage. Warm it all together—bacon pieces and all—and toss it over lettuce."

We rushed home to try it. We had some lettuce in our garden as well as cherry tomatoes, fresh off the vine. Then we hard-boiled a couple of Vittoria's eggs to slice up and throw in. We tossed the bacon-balsamic-sage dressing into the fresh-out-of-the-ground lettuce leaves, mixed in the chunks of tomato, egg, and bacon, and had the makings of a perfect lunch. Add a glass of Grechetto, a light local white wine, and that was it.

We were still lingering over the last of the wine when we heard a car making its way down our dirt road. It was JoJo and Bruce, friends whom we hadn't seen since they went off to Mexico the year before. JoJo and Bruce are our heroes, our inspiration; they live more interesting lives on less money than probably anyone in the world. When their son, Miles, went off to college in New York, they decided to explore other possibilities for themselves. JoJo had been selling real estate, Bruce had been teaching English to the Italian army, and they both felt a need to stretch out a bit. They've been expats for years. They moved to Italy when Miles was in grade school because they thought their life in New York was living them rather than the other way around. They bought a pile of old rocks in a little town outside Spoleto and spent years learning how to make a house out of it. They reinvented themselves. Bruce, who had been an actor and film editor in New York, became adept at plumbing, wiring, masonry, and carpentry, while JoJo, a successful talent agent in their former life, mastered Italian cooking.

Now, with Miles off to college, they decided to go exploring. To finance their travels, they rent their Umbrian house and live off the proceeds. This meant they needed to find a country where they could live cheaply and warmly—JoJo hates the cold. So last year was spent in Mexico and next is to be spent in Vietnam. They're back home in Umbria to get their house spruced up for the new renters and to take part in the summer festivities—they try to never miss a party.

I quickly ran to the fridge to grab another bottle of wine and we put out some olives and pecorino cheese.

"No. Jesus. No wine for us," said JoJo, waving me off. "We just had a big lunch with George and Mariane." Mariane is JoJo's mother; George is her husband.

"How about an *amaro*? Or a little grappa?"

Bruce lit up. "An *amaro* would be nice."

"To settle the stomach," I urged. "JoJo?"

"No. I'll stick to wine. I can't do that sweet stuff in the middle of the day."

And the party continues.

We had been keeping up with their year in Mexico through a Web site that Bruce put together. Every month we—and all their friends—were able to see photos of their latest adventures with witty comments from both of them written underneath.

"Did you actually get gored by that bull?" I asked. "Or was that trick photography?"

"No, that was real," said Bruce. "No trip to Mexico is complete without a goring or two."

"Not for me; that's Bruce's department. He took the goring; I did the cooking."

"How was the food?"

"Quite wonderful, actually. Most people think of Mexican food as that Tex-Mex glop you get in the states, but they have at least as rich a food tradition as Italy. Maybe better. And the cooking is completely different from region to region. I learned a lot."

"So when are you cooking for us?"

"Whenever you want. I'll put up a nice pot of stewed tripe for you. It'll knock your socks off."

She gave me a sweet smile. JoJo loves guts—sweetbreads, tripe, kidneys, brains—all that stuff. I think it comes from her British background. And she knows very well that I can't stomach it.

"So what about you guys?" asked Bruce, taking a sip of his *amaro*. "How was it getting back to New York?"

"Humbling," I said. "We're starting from the beginning again in the theater."

"Old new kids on the block," added Jill.

"But you don't want to work that much anyway, do you?" asked JoJo.

"Not me," I said. "I'd be perfectly happy to retire here and grill pork chops all day. But Jilly still has the itch."

"I do. And I'm working on my singing again. I found a great teacher."

"All right, so this is perfect," says JoJo. "Jill works her ass off, singing and dancing eight shows a week, and Mikey stays home and cooks pork chops. Then when the show closes and you're unemployed, you both come to Italy and party."

"That's more or less the plan," said Jill. "But I've also got my mom to worry about."

"Why? What's wrong with your mother?"

"You know, she's getting old, and her husband's even older. I just feel uncomfortable being, like, eight thousand miles away from her."

"You can go out to see her when you get back from Italy, no?"

"Oh sure. We will. But . . . she seems so vulnerable to me right now and I feel far away. I can't do anything to help her."

"All our moms are vulnerable. They're getting old. It's not about how far away you are. I have those concerns about my mother and I just had lunch with her five minutes ago."

# SEVEN

# Max

OUR SON, MAX, CAME TO STAY FOR A WEEK during
Umbria Jazz, the international jazz festival in Perugia. Max is
a musician, so he moves in circles very different from ours in
New York—and at different times of the day and night. Sometimes weeks can go by without our hearing from him. I think
we've actually seen more of him here in Italy than we do when
we're all back in New York. We tempted him over this time
by getting tickets to some of the events at Umbria Jazz, which
is just forty-five minutes north of us. Whatever gets him here
is fine with us.

Max graduated a couple of years ago from the Jazz
Program at the New School in Greenwich Village. He's a
drummer—and a brilliant one, in my unbiased opinion. He's
usually working with a few different bands at the same time,
often playing rock and roll so that he has some chance of making money out of it. Jazz is pretty much just for love. But he
has gigs on a regular basis in New York. He's making his way
in a tough business—a lot tougher than the acting business,
from what I can see. But he has no choice, it's a calling; he's
been a serious musician since he was eight years old and Jill

took him to see the movie *Amadeus*. When he came home he ran to the bathroom mirror and starting combing his hair like Tom Hulce. He told us he was sure he had been Mozart in a former life. Jill sat him down at the piano and showed him how to pick out a familiar passage from *Eine Kleine Nachtmusik*. A week later he was studying with someone who specialized in teaching kids. A month after that, she came to us and said he needed a better teacher—he was moving too fast for her. Then, sometime around his twelfth birthday, he discovered the drums—his teacher said he'd been playing the piano like a drum set for years—and he was off to his destiny.

It was wonderful to have him in Umbria for a visit. Because he had no car and didn't speak a word of the language, he was our prisoner for a few days, and we took full advantage. We trotted him around to our favorite restaurants and then had a big party at the Rustico so that all our friends could meet him. And in the mornings over breakfast, Jill was able to grill him about his work and his girlfriends. A rock drummer may have to struggle to get work, but girls seem to be in plentiful supply.

Then we all set off to Perugia for the festival. We had tickets to see an afternoon concert by Stefano Bollani, the brilliant Italian jazz pianist, and afterward, Max said he just wanted to hang around Perugia on his own and check out the scene. Besides the scheduled concerts, there were street bands playing everywhere and jam sessions hidden away in the backs of bars. We helped him check into a cheap bed-and-breakfast and left him on his own. He had our phone number if he needed anything.

Jill was a little worried about leaving him, because he spoke no Italian, but I reminded her that he was a grown man now and could fend for himself. These were the same roles we'd been playing since we started the parenting game thirty-some years ago when Alison was a little girl. Jill would nurture and protect; I would urge them to try their wings in the wide world, stand on their own two feet. It's like the good cop–bad cop routine.

I got up early the next morning—as usual—and tiptoed downstairs so as not to wake Jill up. I'd put on some coffee, do my morning crossword puzzle, and then see if I could get some writing done. I walked into the kitchen and there, to my complete shock, was Max, sitting at the kitchen table nursing a cup of coffee and eating a jelly-filled *cornetto*.

"What . . . ? How . . . ?"

He smiled a very self-satisfied grin and said, "I took the train." Then he offered me some coffee, which I gratefully accepted, and he passed me the bag of pastries. A little voice in the back of my head pointed out that he wasn't a kid any more.

"I found a jam session last night. It started at midnight and went until morning. I got a chance to sit in and they wanted me to play most of the night. It's really amazing here. Italian musicians are great."

"What train?" I asked. I was still hung up about how he got here. The closest station was Spoleto, which would still leave him fifteen miles away from us.

"When I got back to the hotel just after the sun came up, it was locked and the bell didn't work." Then he laughed and said that he had called up to the window like Romeo, but no one answered.

"So I went down to the railroad station and there wasn't a train to Spoleto until, like, nine o'clock. But the guy spoke pretty good English and he said there was a local train that leaves really early and stops at all the stops, all the way to Rome—he said it was a milk train. So I took it and before we got to Spoleto, I heard the conductor call out, "Campello" so I got off. Did you know there was a station here?"

I did but I didn't think anybody used it any more. It was all the way down across the Flaminia in a place that nobody goes.

"I was asleep when he called it out and almost missed it."

"So then you walked?" It's around four miles from the station to our house. All uphill.

"Yeah. It's long. I stopped in town on the way to get a coffee and I got these doughnuts for you guys."

"Thanks."

"No problem. It was nice walking in the morning. All those birds singing."

"Yeah, morning's great. You should try it more often."

Max has always been a singular young man. I would say that he marches to his own drummer, except that, of course, he is his own drummer. Around the time we moved out of Los Angeles—Max was then twelve years old—he was diagnosed with a learning disorder, a visual to conceptual problem that made it hard for him to pick things up off the page. Not good for school. He saw a specialist, who was able to correct it to a great degree, but she also said that he had learned to compensate for the problem with his listening ability—his ear—which had become highly sensitized. Very good for a musician. Max hears things that other people aren't aware of—like a dog hears high-pitched whistles that humans can't hear. We were in a department store once and he said, "There's that James Taylor song you love." I didn't even know there was music playing.

He couldn't relate at all to where we were living in Marin County. It was too rich and way too white for his taste, so once he got his driver's license he was off to the East Bay immediately. He hung out in Berkeley first and then found what he was really looking for in Oakland. He went to poetry slams and jam sessions on a regular basis and got to know the local music scene. Two different drummers mentored him—one stressed more classical jazz techniques and the other introduced Max to Latin jazz rhythms. He practiced for hours every day; we had to soundproof his bedroom.

On Sundays he started going to a church in San Francisco—the Saint John Coltrane African Orthodox Church. We had never done anything in the way of religious upbringing with either of our children—I was a bagel-and-cream-cheese Jew, and Jill's parents had brought her up as a Unitarian, which as far as I could figure out meant that you thought a great deal of Ralph Waldo Emerson. Anyway, our kids were left to figure out the whole God thing on their own. So when Max let slip one Sunday that he was late for church, I was one surprised poppa. A few weeks later—when we got over our surprise—we attended the church to see what was going on. There was a preacher, who basically did what preachers do, and there was a band that the congregants were encouraged to join whenever they wanted. People brought their own instruments. I don't think they ever rehearsed; it just kind of happened. Some people played, some listened, some danced or swayed or sang with the music. It was cacophonous; not really pleasant, actually. But I could see how it was powerful—almost hallucinogenic—if you were really into it. Jill and I had to leave after a little while. Too intense. Max would have to be on his own with his religious training.

It was the music that drew him, of course. But Max also had—still has—a spiritual yearning. Around the same time that he was going to the Coltrane church, he joined a Buddhist group and learned to chant. So his religious affiliations were varied, but each one seemed to lead him to some transcendent place.

When he was in college in New York, he went to Lincoln Center to see a concert of sacred music from around the world. There was a group called the McCullough Sons of Thunder from a church in Harlem called the United House of Prayer. It was a gospel trombone choir—seven or eight trombones, a tuba, a rhythm section, and a preacher. A week later Max showed up at the church. He sat there through the nearly three-hour service and then returned Sunday after Sunday until someone asked him what he wanted. When he said he wanted to play with them, he was put on cymbals, and he's been in the band ever since. He went with the group on tour to Morocco, Sweden, the Monterey Jazz Festival, and, last year, Carnegie Hall.

I told Max to hang out a second and I went upstairs to our bedroom. I gently woke Jill.

"What's wrong, honey?"

"Max is downstairs." When she looked worried, I added that everything was fine.

"I just thought you'd like to grab a piece of this."

She put on her robe and came downstairs to the kitchen. I let Max explain the whole story of the jam session and the closed hotel and the milk train to Campello. Jill was most interested in the music, of course. She's a musician in her own right—a piano player and a superb singer—and she always regretted not going into music professionally. But she has a son who's living her dream, not unlike how Alison was living out my fantasy of being a professional chef.

"These guys were great players," he told her. "They didn't speak English and I couldn't speak Italian and it didn't matter at all. We talked all night."

Transcendent.

"Did they like your playing?" Jill knew the answer to that; Max is an awesome player.

"Yeah, they were like . . . so supportive, I couldn't believe it. I'm used to that jam session I go to in Harlem, where everybody's critical and competitive. But these guys were like my family. They wanted me to be good."

Jill was in heaven, eating up every crumb of this rare moment with her son. Her eyes were like a kid's at a birthday party, just before the candles get blown out. They talked on and on about the music; at one point, Max banged out a riff in six/eight time on the kitchen table as Jill nibbled away on a jelly doughnut. If it had gone on any longer, I thought, she'd be drinking coffee.

# EIGHT

# Guests

THE ITALIAN WORD FOR GUEST IS *ospite*. It's also the word for host. So when you're talking about having people over, it's sometimes hard to tell who's pitching and who's catching. But I think the Italians are on to something—that maybe you shouldn't be a guest in someone's house until you've been on the other side, hosting people at your place.

We had our first *ospiti* of the summer coming in a couple of days—two couples, old, dear friends whom we couldn't wait to see. David and Susan Liederman, who have been our friends for thirty years; and Lynne Meadow and Ron Shechtman, who go back even further. Lynne and Jill went to drama school together. We all did a trip to India together—joined at the hip for sixteen days of squalor, disease, and diarrhea. If you can get through that and still be friends, you can do anything. It's funny about guests; they can be either the very best thing that happens to your summer or the worst.

Now, before I get into my diatribe about the worst, let me admit that I am my own biggest problem when it comes to having unwanted people in my house. I am an inveterate, compulsive, serial inviter. I have been known to invite entire roomfuls of strangers all at once. We were at a book signing at a Barnes and Noble in Chicago once, there were maybe 150 people listening to us talk about our house in Italy, and I blurted out, "Hey guys, come on over—you only live once— we'll be there all summer." I thought it was funny at the time.

I've invited the wine delivery guy, my Korean dry cleaner and his family, a couple of girls sitting at a bar—it doesn't matter if I know people or like them; it has nothing to do with them, really. I've invited whole tables of people I meet in restaurants; I always invite waiters, for some rea- son—instead of giving a big tip, I guess. Fortunately, most of these people don't take me seriously. And if they did and actually wanted to show up at our house, I would just blame it on Jill.

"Hey, who are these assholes? Come on, honey, I don't want these people in my house."

Then there's a special category of unwanted guests—the ones who want to come so badly that they preempt the invi- tation. "We're coming to visit you in Italy this summer! We're doing it! We booked the flight." And no one ever asked them.

"*Che palle,*" as the Italians would say. What balls.

Invariably they're the ones who let you know—at the last minute—that they're afraid to drive in a foreign country, and also that the trains are too confusing. "Everything's in a foreign language!" Imagine. This means we're expected to drive two hours to pick them up at the airport in Rome, and drive them back when they finally leave. Worst of all, it means they'll be tied to us hand and foot the entire time they're with us; with- out a car, they'll hardly be able to pee without our holding their hand. But that's fine with them—they don't want to see the sights without us, we're the reason they came; they want to soak up every second they can with us. "But," we want to tell them, "we barely know you. And we've already been to Assisi." Many, many times.

They want to stay for weeks, of course. What's the point of coming all that way unless you spend some time? They don't understand that we have things to do when we're not washing their sheets and towels.

"You have to see Venice," we say. "And Florence," urging them out the door.

"No, no," they reply. "That's much too expensive. The hotels alone. And we'd much rather be with you."

They bring a gift. A tchotchke. As if that would forgive their boorish intrusion; as if that would offset their blatant theft of a week or more of our precious and rapidly diminishing life. Jill doesn't want me to write anything bad about the gifts, because we've gotten some lovely ones. Okay. Thank you all for the lovely ones. But really—come on, guys, don't you think if we needed a salad bowl we would have bought one by now? One that we actually like?

Okay. Enough. Calm down. We've also had many good guests, some very good guests, and best of all, a few positively brilliant guests—people that make the summer and ultimately enrich our lives. One couple—old friends—e-mailed ahead of their visit, "Don't make any plans; we have a surprise for you." The day after they arrived, they whisked us off for a three-day vacation on the beach in Le Marche. Brilliant. So remember when you're reading this, when I talk about those overbearing, self-serving, inconceivably boring guests, I'm not talking about you. We loved having you. I'm talking about those other people.

The Shechtmans and the Liedermans are in the category of great guests. Obviously. Otherwise I wouldn't be talking about them in this chapter. Maybe the most important element is that we can all just be who we are and what we are and nobody feels the need to pretend otherwise. There's no forced conviviality, no politeness; and we laugh a lot.

We decided to plan a very special evening for the Saturday after they arrived. The Spoleto festival was in full swing, so Jill and I drove into town to see if we could get tickets for a concert. We parked at the bottom of the hill; when the festival's happening, it's impossible to park up top. We hiked up to the Piazza della Libertà and got six tickets for a symphony concert that would take place in the piazza in front of the *duomo,* the magnificent Spoleto cathedral. We would hear the Saint Petersburg Symphony Orchestra—not the one from Tampa, the Russian one. We had attended a similar concert there the year before and it was a knockout. The concert started at dusk. You could see the green Umbrian hills in the background behind the cathedral catching the dying rays of the sun. The orchestra hit the first notes and little birds— hundreds and hundreds of them, startled out of their resting place in the bell tower—filled the air around the cathedral and square-danced in time to the music. We wanted our friends to experience that.

After we secured the tickets, we walked up the hill to a favorite restaurant of ours, just off the Piazza Mercato. It's called Il Tempio del Gusto and it's run by a lovely young couple—Manuela runs the front of the house and Eros is the chef. We stopped in to say hi and to make a reservation for Saturday; the plan was to eat there after the concert, around 10:30—very Italian. The restaurant was empty when we looked in. It was only around 7:30, and the place wouldn't fill up until around nine at the earliest. After we made the reservation, Manuela asked us if we'd like to sit and have a glass of *prosecco,* and after the slightest bit of arm-twisting we said okay. We had no plans that evening.

With the *prosecco,* Manuela brought out a plate of olives and a platter of house-made salami, each slice delicately wrapped around a filling of truffle paste. This was bar food of a very high order. She filled my glass again; Jill's had been barely touched. We munched a bit and talked about what else we'd do with our guests when they got here. And then Eros came out with plate of fritto misto—zucchini flowers, sage leaves, and basil leaves dipped in the lightest batter and flash-fried. He also put down a small dish of sea salt, so that we could sprinkle a bit on just before we popped them into our mouths. They were seducing us into dinner, and we didn't put up much resistance. They're seductive people.

I had pasta first—big surprise—homemade tagliatelle in a duck *ragù.* Jill started with a salad. I admired her restraint but at the same time I felt she was missing out on a serious bowl of pleasure. Eros has a way with duck. There's never a drop of grease in it, and yet it's full of taste. Long, slow, cooking is the answer, I think. And some aged *balsamico.* The duck gets a chance to caramelize in the pot so that the already sweet flesh gets even sweeter and the skin crisps up and turns a dark copper color. So you twirl the fresh-egg pasta strands around in the caramelized duck sauce and then, just before you put it into your mouth, you top the forkful off with a crispy, crackly piece of skin. Oh, Mama.

Jilly thoroughly relished her leaves.

Then we split a plate of Eros's osso buco, which is a specialty. I don't know what he does to make it so much better than other people's, except that the ingredients are so perfectly fresh. Carrots, celery, and onion—the great Italian trilogy—slowly braised with the shanks, some wine, some tomato, and a little fresh thyme, I think, until the meat, the vegetables, and the juices all meld into each other and become something else entirely. Manuela opened a bottle of Montefalco Rosso, a local red that I've grown very fond of. If I walked out of the restaurant and went to the top of the hill, I could see where the grapes in this wine grow. It's right over there. It's as local as the veal and the carrots and the thyme. They all grew up in the same neighborhood, they went to the same elementary school, their families have known each other for generations, and this is why they go down so well together. Good food and drink are no mystery. You just can't cheat.

The restaurant started to fill up and I caught Manuela's eye. We had walked in without a reservation and the place has only twelve or so tables. We should hurry up and make room for the real customers. But she smiled and waved me off. "Take your time," she was saying. "The table is yours for the night."

Okay. Then we got into some serious lingering. Lingering is an Italian art form, virtually unknown on the other side of the Atlantic. In the states, you finish your meal, you get the check, you leave. In Italy, the meal doesn't ever really end; there's always one more thing, a little taste of this or that, a bit of fruit, a cookie, coffee. Then there's the *digestivo*—an alcoholic beverage designed to help you digest your meal. You've got to love these people—they not only want to feed you; they want to help you digest it as well. We had the table for almost four hours before we tottered out of there to find our car and head home.

We walked the slow way to the bottom of the hill, spiraling slowly down through the narrow cobblestone streets. Spoleto is a beauty of a town, at the same time ancient and vibrantly alive. I had my arm around Jill. We were full and happy.

I was tired by the time we got home. Too much good food and wine. I headed upstairs to bed while Jill went outside to the pergola to make her nightly call to her mother. The cell phone reception was better out there. I got into bed and read a bit of my book until I got drowsy enough for sleep, and then, just after I turned out the light, I heard Jill calling me from downstairs.

"I'm in bed already," I called down in response.

She said something else that I couldn't quite hear. Jesus.

"What is it, baby?" I called down with a bit of edge in my voice. Once I'm on the sleep track, I hate to be woken up.

She said something again and I still couldn't make it out. I think she wanted to know if I had opened a window or something. Finally I gave up; I threw on a robe and padded down the steps.

"What?" I said in not too nice a tone. "I'm in bed."

"Ralph died."

# NINE

# Santa Barbara

RALPH HAD HAD A SERIES OF SMALL STROKES, each one debilitating him further until he was moved into the skilled nursing facility at the retirement community. Every day Lora sat at his bedside and watched him slowly and steadily disappear. Every night she was on the phone with Jill, ranting about the doctors and about the morphine that was taking him away from her. Alix, who was hanging pretty tight at this point, persuaded Lora to take a break from her vigil and take a walk on her favorite beach, where she and Ralph had spent many afternoons. They were there, watching the pelicans, when Jill got the call from Josie that Ralph was gone. That was the call she received while I was upstairs grumbling about trying to get to sleep.

At that point, everyone knew about Ralph's death except Lora and Alix. Jill reached Alix on her cell phone at the beach and—out of Lora's earshot—suggested she drive back to the apartment where Lora had her special phone for the hearing impaired and Jill would break the news to her there.

While we waited for them to drive home, I called the airline to see when we could get a flight. It was the high season and there wasn't much available. I kept using the words "funeral" and "death" and "father" until they found us a couple of seats. We left the return open because we didn't quite know what kind of situation we were going to find when we got there. We called the kids and made plans for them to meet us in Santa Barbara. Max, who was coming from New York, said he'd like to use the trip as an opportunity to see friends in Los Angeles, and Alison said he could stay with her for the week. She said she'd make sure that they got to all the appropriate gatherings in Santa Barbara. It felt good to see our kids developing this relationship as adults. They're twelve years apart and never saw much of each other when they were young.

Then Jill called Lora at her apartment.

"Hi, Mom, it's me." A pause. "Honey, Ralph died. I just heard from Josie that he's gone." She listened for a moment and then indicated to me that Lora was crying.

"It's what he wanted, Mom. He was in such terrible pain."

Now Jill was crying with her and nodding.

"Yes. He's been released. The pain is over now."

Jill told her that Kathy, Ralph's daughter, was already on her way and that we would be there the following day. Then Jill spoke to Alix, who said that Lora was holding up well and that Frankie and other friends were around her to support her.

"I should be there," Jill said after she hung up.

"Soon, baby. We'll be there soon."

She nodded as if to say that wasn't good enough.

"How is she?"

Jill slowly shook her head.

"She apologized to me for crying."

I made my Jewish shrug that says, *Why do people give themselves such a hard time?*

"She wants to be like Jackie Kennedy."

I shrugged again. This one said, *I'm way out of my depth.*

"She was at her sister Ethel's funeral and she let go a little tear in the car when they were driving away from the cemetery. When she told me about it, she chastised herself. She said she should be like Jackie Kennedy—silent and strong in her grief."

"And well dressed."

"Sure."

I don't think I've mentioned yet that Lora has always been a beautiful woman; she still is. But—like her beautiful daughter—she has always been concerned with what people think of her, obsessed, if you will, with her image, with how she's coming over. And—as with her beautiful daughter—this need to create a *bella figura* often got in the way of her ability to experience the moment. As every good actor knows, you can't watch yourself and be yourself at the same time.

Jill has spent her adult life working on this issue. Just becoming an actor was the beginning; by putting on the mask of a character she felt free to express herself. Then, with a long list of disciplines over the years—therapy, yoga, meditation, feminist workshops, tantric sex courses with her husband—she learned to actually free herself, be herself, without putting on a mask. Jill has a passion for self-improvement, a genius for change and growth, a keen appetite for experiencing the moment. Her mom could learn a lot from her.

"They really loved each other, I think."

"Yeah," I agreed. "In their way. They got married a year before we did. So, they had what, thirty-four years?"

Jill nodded and we thought for a moment about their thirty-four years together. Sure, they fought a lot. Like my parents. They seemed to feel that by putting each other down, they were raising themselves up. Jill and I have learned the hard way over the years that it doesn't work that way—when one goes down, you both go down. But Ralph and Lora were from another generation. They did things the way they did things.

"Here's to Ralph," I said, lifting an imaginary glass. Jill did the same and we clinked to Ralph.

"The Liedermans are getting on a plane in half an hour," I reminded her.

"Oh, my God. And Lynne and Ron."

"They're already in London. I have no idea how to get in touch with them."

"What are we going to do?"

"We're going to welcome them, maybe have dinner with them tomorrow night, and then say good-bye. What else can we do?"

I could see that Jill was having a hard time with this. She had been especially excited about having Lynne as a guest. I decided not to point out that the day after the Liedermans and Shechtmans left, Alix, who's been taking such good care of Jill's mom in Santa Barbara, would arrive for a three-day visit with her son and Jake, her new boyfriend. This was tough because we had virtually insisted they come here first before they went on to Florence and Rome—so that we could personally welcome them to Italy and make them feel at home. Now we weren't even going to be here.

"I feel terrible about this," she said.

I just looked at her.

"How can we just walk out on our guests like that? They're coming all this way."

Okay. So despite all the therapy, the years of meditation, the thousands upon thousands of yoga postures, she was caught like a mouse on one of those sticky-paper traps. Should she show up well to her mother and her mothers' friends? Or should she show up well to the Shechtmans and the Liedermans? The shiksa's dilemma.

"We'll go to your mom."

She nodded and kept thinking, her feet still stuck to the trap.

"And the Shechtmans and the Liedermans will understand."

A pause.

"Oh, God. Then Alix is coming."

Clink. The penny drops.

Actually, the Liedermans had stayed at the house before—on their own. They were thinking about buying a house themselves and we offered them ours as a base while they were looking. They knew how everything in the house worked and didn't work. They could entertain Ron and Lynne while we ran off to take care of Jill's mom. Then, on their way out, they could welcome Alix and her brood, show them where the bedrooms are and everything. We should put them on staff.

"We'll miss the concert at the *duomo.*"

I nodded. Worse, we'd miss the dinner afterward at Il Tempio del Gusto. That was hard. There'd always be another concert.


There was no funeral. Ralph was cremated as specified in his will, and there was a memorial service later in the week at the retirement community. Kathy and Jill, along with Frankie and Tap and some of their other friends, helped Lora plan the service. Jill suggested that Lora read a letter and poem that she had sent to Ralph on his ninetieth birthday, other friends read poems and gave remembrances, the kids told Grandpa

stories, I was the master of ceremonies. The Buddhist nun was
there. Although she hadn't worked out as a companion for
Lora—it seems she was so soft-spoken that Lora couldn't
understand a word she said—her calm presence at the service was a nice touch. We spent a moment with Alix and Jake,
who were leaving the following day to stay with us in Italy. We
had arranged for the Liedermans to welcome them as they
were heading out and, hopefully, we'd be there a few days later
to be proper hosts. Jake took me aside and told me—in confidence—that he would be asking Alix to marry him the night
they arrived at our house. They would not be the first ones;
the Rustico has a long history—long before we owned it—of
inspiring engagements, weddings, and many, many consum-
mations of weddings.

After the service, everyone had lunch in the dining
room, and that was the end of it. Lora was composed and
thoughtful at the service, elegantly put together in a purple
suit and lavender blouse. Afterward, at the luncheon, she
graciously spoke with each person individually, taking care
to thank everyone for his or her support. She was dazzling.
She was Jackie Kennedy.

I sat there, pushing a dry piece of chicken around my
plate, and flashed on the funerals I'd experienced in my family. My dad was one of fifteen kids, my mother one of seven,
so there were a lot of deaths over the years. In my family,
people cried at funerals. And I don't mean just a little tear
appearing at the corner of an eye; I mean moaning, keening,
the beating of breasts, mournful angry questions to God: "Why
me? How could you do this to me? He was so young. He was
so good. How could you take him from me?"

No matter that the rabbi tried to put a philosophical
tone on the whole thing: "Mysterious are the ways of

God . . ." My family didn't buy that crap for a second. They wanted answers.

And afterward? There was no dry little luncheon where everyone murmured kind thoughts. My family ate for seven fucking days. Stuffed themselves. People brought huge platters from the delicatessen. Some were meat-oriented—corned beef, roast beef, pastrami, tongue, and chopped liver, with loaves of sliced seeded-rye bread, mustard, and coleslaw. Some were fish-oriented—lox, nova, herring in cream sauce with onions, and sturgeon, along with bagels, cream cheese, sliced tomatoes, and onions. There were giant urns for coffee, and plates of cookies, coffee cake, and fruit-filled pastries. The widow and the sisters of the deceased worked like slaves to keep the food coming—putting out new plates and silverware, washing the old plates and silverware, combining the platters so that there was enough room on the groaning table. This is how my family mourned the dead.

We met with Kathy about the financial situation. She had been paying their bills and handling whatever else needed to be done, but now that Ralph was gone, we all agreed that the responsibility should fall to us. Kathy suggested that we get Lora to sign a power of attorney for Jill as Ralph had done for her. The most difficult job would be handling all her medical insurance forms, but Alix had been doing that for Lora and said she wouldn't mind continuing. At what we thought was a proper moment, Jill and I tried to speak with Lora about money. We wanted to reassure her that she was covered and that we would be available to help her with everything and that she needn't worry. But she demurred. Jackie Kennedy doesn't talk about money at times like this.

We met with Frankie, who was Lora's closest friend. She assured us that she would organize lots of dinner invitations for Lora in the main dining room; different groups of friends would take turns having her at their table. This community had a lot of experience with widowhood, and people knew how to reintegrate someone gently into the swim of things. Before Ralph had become so sick, Lora was involved in a lot of activities—the choir, watercolors in the art studio, the book club, the Unitarian church. Now her friends would urge her back to all these things and more.

On the weekend, there was a barbecue on the main lawn. It featured a Dixieland band—all the players were over eighty—lots of food and drink, and a beautiful southern California afternoon. Jill and I persuaded Lora to let us squire her to the party. After a few moments of obligatory bereaved behavior, Lora got engaged in a discussion about the Save the Sand Hill Cranes Project and she was off and running. I thought that I hadn't seen her so energized in a long time. Jill had been right—Ralph's decline and eventual demise had been a terrible drain on her, and now we were seeing a significant rebound, both mental and physical.

We met with Josie. After our last visit, when Josie had made her pitch for the dementia ward, Jill had fired off an indignant letter to her, insisting that Josie had greatly exaggerated Lora's problems. Now the two of them were dancing around each other, each trying to concede the other's position.

"She seems to be doing so well, Jill. You were right. Your mom is a long way from going into Elmview."

"But I've seen the behavior that you're talking about. She's definitely forgetting a lot and . . . well, there's always been a streak of paranoia. Who knows? Elmview could be a wonderful place for her eventually."

My only experience with dementia was with my mom. She died of Alzheimer's disease. I hadn't realized you could die of that, but it seems that eventually the brain just forgets to give signals to the major organs and the body shuts down. That's what happened with my mother. But Lora didn't look to me as if she had Alzheimer's. She forgot things, but nothing like my mom, who could misplace her purse every thirty seconds.

"Where's my bag?"

"It's right here, Mom." I hand it to her, she puts it on the table.

"What were we talking about?" she asks.

I tell her.

"Where's my bag?" Panic in her eyes.

"Here it is, Mom." I hand it to her, she puts it back on the table.

"What were we talking about?"

Lora was nothing like that. Whatever she's suffering from is different from what my mom had.

Jill tells Josie that Frankie will be organizing Lora's social life, and Josie assures her that the community will be very supportive.

"We're her family," she tells Jill, giving her a sisterly hug.

The next day we took Lora out to lunch at a nice place in Santa Barbara. She mentioned that she had called about going back to work as a volunteer for the League of Women Voters. We booked our flight back to Italy.

## TEN

# Walking on Eggs

"She's going to be okay."

I nodded. Our plane for Italy had just taken off and this was the eighth time Jill had said that her mom was going to be okay. But I was right with her—I thought Lora was doing great, too. I was feeling very optimistic. She hadn't looked so good in years. Whoops, that's four times for me. Let's get real— Lora's eighty-seven, she's blacking out for no good reason and she had thought her husband of thirty-four years was having sex with some guy in a van. How okay could she be? I settled into my seat to face yet another twelve-hour flight. If the truth be told, I was actually more concerned about my hemorrhoids than I was about Lora.

Alix, Talon, and Jake were waiting for us when we got to the Rustico. Alix and Jake had managed to get themselves engaged a few nights before, without our help, and they were all gushy about it. Jake was adorable, actually—as if he were the first person ever to come up with the idea of getting engaged. I think he wanted us to put a plaque in the guest bedroom to immortalize the moment. Talon seemed quite happy about the whole thing, too. He and Jake got on well, so the

new family looked solid. We took them out to the Palazzaccio
to celebrate, and the next day they were off to Florence: this
made them—after the Liedermans and the Shechtmans—the
easiest guests we've ever had.

The next night Joe and Teresa threw a party to celebrate
our return from Ralph's funeral. They've had a house in
Umbria for years and they also have an apartment three blocks
away from us in New York City, so we've been getting to be
very close friends. Joe makes me smile—like no one I've ever
met. Every time I run into him or talk with him on the phone,
I find myself grinning like an idiot—like the night he arrived
in Italy this summer and called me from the car.

"Michele, we're a half hour out. Can you meet us at Dei
Pini? If you get there first, order, we'll be right behind you.
I'm not going home, I'm not unpacking, I'm diving straight
off the highway into a bowl of *strangozzi tartufo*. I need it,
Michele. It's like a drug."

We call each other by our Italian names—like six-year-olds.

"Giuseppe, *stai calmo*. You'll have an accident. Let Teresa
drive."

"You haven't left the house yet? Come on, man, don't let
me down. Don't make me eat all that pasta by myself."

Teresa tells a story about Joe that gives you some idea of
the size of his heart. They had guests visiting them from the
states—cousins of Teresa, a whole family, who had never been
to a foreign country before. After a week at Joe and Teresa's
house, it was time for the cousins to move on to Florence,
Venice, and Rome. But Joe sensed that they were nervous
about traveling, so he offered to go with them and be their
tour guide through the rest of their stay. He drove them,
booked their hotels, found the best trattorias, and guided
them around the various cities until they were ready to go

home. Then he drove them to the airport and waved them off. And these were her cousins, not his.

Teresa's a caution, too. But in a different way. Whereas Joe is full frontal with his approach, Teresa's on the sly side. She does herself up like a schoolteacher—severe glasses, prim dresses, sensible shoes. But none of this even barely conceals the fact that she's a total babe. Joe's crazy about her. He's a one-gal guy and she's the gal.

The main reason they threw the party, other than to welcome us back from Santa Barbara, was to plan yet another party for the feast of San Lorenzo, which is a yearly event on August 10. It's also called, famously, the Night of the Shooting Stars. In prior years, the whole bunch would drive to the Piano Grande beyond the Valnerina. This is a vast, flat plain three thousand meters above sea level and a perfect place to watch shooting stars. Bruce would cook on a makeshift barbecue and then everyone would sleep under the stars in sleeping bags— except all those who were too old or too intelligent to want to wake up at dawn encased in a block of ice; these people went to a nearby hotel instead. It gets cold at three thousand meters, even in August.

So this year, JoJo had another idea: We would have a party—again—at Joe and Teresa's house, which was at a high enough elevation to watch the meteor shower. But first we would all perform—with scripts in hand—the third act of *As You Like It,* which, as JoJo pointed out, was about another insane group of people frolicking on a summer night. By the time JoJo had proposed this, we had all had enough wine to agree, so the plan was adopted. JoJo would cast the parts and we would all be responsible for bringing our own costumes.

Jill was excited because she would get to play Rosalind, which is one of the world's great roles for an actress. I would play Touchstone, the fool. No comment. The other parts were argued over and finally decided upon, with JoJo making the final decisions. Joe would play Phoebe—in drag, of course. Teresa would hang back and observe the rest of us making fools of ourselves. She's a photographer by profession, an observer by temperament.

Later, after the party to plan the party, we slowly drove home from Joe and Teresa's house and performed our nightly ritual: Jill called her mom and I went up to bed. I was all tucked in and reading my book when Jill came upstairs. She had taken longer than usual.

"Everything okay?"

"No. I've been on the phone with Frankie and then Meg, trying to arrange play dates for my mom. Nobody's been inviting her to dinner."

"I thought that was all taken care of."

"I thought so too. But Mom just told me that she's been eating alone every night over in the assisted-care dining room. So I made some calls. Meg, at least, had the courtesy to tell me the truth."

"Which is?"

"It's hard for them. She talks too much and too loud, she keeps changing the subject, and it drives people crazy. They have a life to lead, too."

"That's her hearing, isn't it?"

"I guess so. But maybe it's her memory problem, too. I don't know. It was easier when Ralph was there to help her."

"He covered for her. He didn't want her to look bad."

She nodded. "I miss Ralph. I don't think I ever really appreciated him until now. Even if he was critical of her and had to do everything by the rules, he took care of her. He really did. And now she has to go to those dinners on her own, and she doesn't know how to do it any more."

She sighed a big one.

"I've been trying to get people to like my mom . . . since I was little kid."

She started to cry. No sound, just fat tears rolling down, her face painted with sadness.

"All my boyfriends. None of them ever got her. You, too."

I knew this was right. My hackles went up whenever I got around Lora. But I'm an actor; I pretended to like her.

"My dad. He told me later that he hadn't loved her for ten years before he left."

"How about you?"

She looked at me with what I thought was fear.

"Did you like her?"

The tears were really coming now.

"She's my mom."

I nodded and took her hand.

"I had to believe that we had this great relationship. That's why I sold her so hard to other people—if I wanted them to like me, they had to see how wonderful she was. But she talked too much. She thought if she could quote these intelligent things from books and dress well and accessorize well, she'd be well thought of."

"When you sell something that hard, people resist."

She nodded and cried more.

"I kept wanting her to be different. Like other moms. I kept hoping that if I was honest and open with her and spoke slowly into her left ear, she would really understand me and we could have . . . you know . . . an intimate relationship. But she never really heard what I said. She was too tied up with making an impression. Even on me."

"She's the mother you got, baby."

She nodded.

"I wanted a different mother, too," I said. "But Santa never got my letters."

My mom. In her eighties—after she was deep into Alzheimer's disease—she was diagnosed with borderline personality disorder. In fact, she had crossed over that border many years before.

There were similarities between her and Lora. They were both small women from large families; both had big ambitions that were ultimately thwarted; each had an outsize need to make a big impression. But if Lora wanted to be Jackie Kennedy in public, my mom needed to be Auntie Mame. It was as if she'd had too much to drink except that she hadn't. She always started out okay—a little too big, a little too grand, but okay. Then the madness started to creep in. My dad, my brother, and I knew what was coming next—total destruction of the party—and we knew nothing short of a tank could stop her. I can't count the number of weddings, bar mitzvahs, and Passover seders that were sent down in flames by my little Mama. It would always start with some perceived slight, so small that people laughed at its inconsequentiality—a tempest in a teapot, they would laugh. But my mom would worry it like a canker sore until it throbbed, and then more until it bled. Then it got personal; everyone was her enemy; old, ugly things were shouted. Total destruction.

Years later, when Alison was getting married in Los Angeles, we decided to fly my mother out for the wedding. It was a difficult decision because at that point her Alzheimer's was getting very bad and she didn't do well with travel. But my brother, who would also be at the wedding, consulted with her doctor—a psychiatrist—who gave him a pill, just one pill, to give my mother in case she got difficult at the party.

Sure enough, during the wedding dinner, my Aunt Margie, who had the difficult job of babysitting my mother, rushed over to our table.

"Mike, you have to come. Your mother's not happy."

"Not happy with what?"

"She thinks she should be at the head table with the bride and groom."

"No, she's at the grandparents' table. She's in the right place."

"She doesn't think so," said Aunt Margie with an ominous look in her eye.

I ran over to check out the situation and I could see in a flash that my mom was winding up for a big blow. I ran over to my brother.

"Where's the pill? I need the pill!"

He handed me a rather large, lozenge-shaped pill and I ran back to Mom's table.

"Here," I said, handing her the pill. "Take this."

She looked at the pill with contempt.

"This is not my medication. I'm not taking that."

"Mom, it's your pill. You have to take it." I was starting to panic.

"Are you trying to poison me?" She was shouting now. "Is that what this is? Poison?"

Just then an actor walked by and my mom thought she recognized him.

"Is that . . . ?"

And in that moment she forgot her whole previous drama, noticed the pill in her hand, and happily swallowed it down. Ten minutes later she was on the dance floor doing the fox-trot with the head of Paramount.

We sat there on the bed, remembering stories about my mother, and it helped. The tears stopped and Jill actually laughed a bit. Compared with my mom, Lora was Mrs. Cleaver.

"She makes a great impression at first. People are really impressed when they first meet her."

"Sure, she's beautiful and she's a stylish dresser."

"She presents well."

"And she knows everything there is to know about John Muir."

"If life were first impressions, she'd be doing great."

"She's adapting to being alone, and that's tough. But I think she'll make it."

"I think so, too."

Jill likes things to be okay, and that's fine when there's something to be done. But in a situation like this with her mother, where there are no happy solutions—Lora is aging and ailing, and there's nothing Jill can do to slow the process —then she finds a way to pretend it's all okay. She had lost it on the phone with Meg and Frankie and everything was bleak for a moment, but now she was working her way back to the sweet lies that were the basis of her denial system—that every-thing was fine, that Lora would go to work for the League of Women Voters, that her friends would rally around her, that she'd meet another guy and live happily ever after. Anything, anyone, to take the responsibility off her shoulders, where it's been weighing since she was a child.

# ELEVEN

# The Goose Sagra

THE FOLLOWING WEEK WE WERE IN THE BACKSEAT of
Bruce and JoJo's car, heading for the goose sagra in Bettona.
Bruce was driving and JoJo was swiveled around, facing us in
the backseat so that we could get the full brunt of her wisdom.

"Bettona is pretty much the only Etruscan town this side
of the Tiber. There are large sections of the old Etruscan wall
that are still standing."

"Just tell us about the goose."

"No," said Jill. "I want to hear the history."

JoJo smiled beneficently at her.

"As I was saying." She shot me a look of disdain. "All the
towns east of the Tiber were Umbrian except, for some reason, Bettona. So they've got some beautiful Etruscan artifacts."

"You never hear about Umbrian artifacts," mused Bruce.
"Why is that?"

"I think, compared with the Etruscans, the Umbrians were
low-class schnorrers," answered JoJo. "No one wants their
artifacts."

There are sagras all over this area; pretty much every
weekend you can find one. A few miles east of Bettona is

Canarra, where there is a famous onion *sagra*. Assisi has a cherry *sagra*; Santa Maria degli Angeli has a wild boar *sagra*. The idea is to eat the local specialty, cooked and served by the townfolk, and raise money for the local *comune*.

"The Bettona *sagra* used to be *porchetta,* but some time in the eighties they changed it to goose. There are *porchetta* sagras all over the place."

"They decided it was time to honor the local poultry," added Bruce.

"And there's nothing quite like tucking into a big hunk of Bettona roast goose. It's one of the highlights of the summer," said JoJo.

"But watch out for the line cutters. It's an Italian tradition and in Bettona it's been raised to an art form. There are two lines—one to order the food and the other for wine. And they're right next to each other, so sometimes it's hard to figure out who's in which line. So the line cutters loiter in between and the minute you're not looking—usually just before you get up to the cashier—there are five people in front of you who weren't there before."

"That surprises me," said Jill. "Italians are usually so polite."

"They are, but this is more about breaking the rules. Italians have great disdain for regulations—especially if they come from some kind of central government."

"That's why it's so hard to get Italians to pay their taxes," chipped in JoJo.

"Or drive at the speed limit," continued Bruce. "Germans, on the other hand, crave regulations; if there were no line, the Germans would form one—just to feel comfortable."

The evening was a dazzler. It had rained on and off all day, but around seven it started to clear and big, fluffy, pink- and orange-tinted clouds paraded across the sky, like those in a

Renaissance painting. We were on a little country road driving through fields of hay that had been recently cut and stacked into giant wheels. The sun was shooting in at a sideways angle just before it set behind the mountains and its light was literally golden. I felt as if we were making our way through a big bowl of chestnut honey.

We had to park about half a mile away from town in a farmer's field that was set up as a parking lot. Bettona is a hill town set high above the Umbrian plain, and we hiked up along with hundreds of others, sharpening our appetites. Joe and Teresa had gotten there early and found us seats together at one end of a long picnic table covered with a paper tablecloth. Our party was fourteen in all and we took up a little more than half the table. At the other end was a motorcycle gang that had driven in from Arezzo. The two groups eyed each other warily as we dispatched our emissaries to order the food and drink. Sophie, our landscaper, and her husband, Jeffrey, who's a painter, collected all the money and orders and went to the food line while Jim and I hit the wine line. Jim's a poet who lives in Minnesota, and he and his wife have had an apartment in Spoleto for many years. They're among the earliest members of the expat community here in Umbria, but we were just getting to know them. This summer was the first time we were all in the same place at the same time.

The lines were even more chaotic than Bruce had described. There were at least seven that I could see—if people didn't like the length of a line, they just started another one right next to it. But there was no pushing or shoving; everyone was in good humor and we knew we'd get our food eventually.

Once the wine arrived, the two factions at our table became clearly defined. On our end, we were proceeding graciously and decorously toward tipsy conviviality; on the motorcycle end they were standing on the table, chugging whole liters of wine and chanting the name of the local soccer team over and over.

"I think they're having more fun than we are," said Michael. He's also a painter and his wife, Carol, is a photographer.

"I think they're on to something," said Joe, and he went down to their end of the table with a bottle of wine and started chanting and chugging. We all tried it, and it was really amusing for about thirty seconds. The motorcycle gang turned out to be a nice bunch of Italian kids dressed up as hooligans. *Hooliganini,* I guess you could call them. The food arrived and saved the day—it's impossible to chant and eat gnocchi with goose sauce at the same time.

The meal was simple, but ample: antipasto of bruschetta topped with olive oil and various kinds of local salami; then pasta—either gnocchi or tagliatelle—bathed in a rich sauce of goose meat slowly simmered with onion, carrot, celery, garlic, and red wine until it blends into a *ragù.* Then the star of the evening, goose, hot-roasted in a wood oven—as simple as that, no frills, no sauce, no rubs, maybe a little salt and pepper. Then came a big plate of grilled vegetables for the more health-conscious among us. The *hooliganini* had no grilled vegetables. They were devouring their goose with their hands, but before we could get judgmental about that, we noticed that the people at all the other tables were doing the same. So—down went the cutlery. It was a six-napkin event.

At around 10:30 or eleven, the dinner started breaking up and people took to wandering around Bettona. All the stores were open for the sagra and there was rumored to be dancing at the big piazza. Our gang split in half with the guys—and JoJo—heading for a bar for grappa, and the girls going off on their own to check out the dancing.

The bar was small and the front door was open to let in some of the evening breeze. JoJo, once she had her glass of grappa, decided to sit on the steps outside and savor the cigar Bruno had given her. This was apparently a tradition with them at the Bettona goose sagra. Our group was half in the bar, half out on the steps, and we watched the sagra revelers snaking their way through the crooked, ancient streets, shopping, singing, and walking off their dinners.

After a while, the girls showed up—in a jolly mood indeed. There had been no dancing, because of some kind of construction in the piazza, so they had gone on a shopping spree instead. Actually, it was more of a gambling spree. A staple at a sagra is the *pesca di beneficenza,* roughly translated as "fishing for charity." You pay one euro to fish around in a bowl filled with folded-up pieces of paper with numbers written on them. Then you hand your number to a pair of old women dressed in black and they look it up on a list and tell you what you've won—or haven't won. Usually the prizes are cheap little plastic things—like a whistle or letter opener—but sometimes you can win something of actual value. When that happens, the old women start shrieking and running around, yelling, "*La pesca, la pesca!*" at the top of their lungs. That means you won the big fish. All the girls had won some prize or other but Jill was the big winner, with six matching wineglasses.

"Antique wineglasses," boasted Jill, meaning that they were used and chipped.

By the time the girls arrived at the bar, they were in a deep discussion about—what else?—aging parents, of course. Jill was the seminar leader, but Mayes and Sophie were going through similar problems with their mothers and then Joe pitched in with a story about his dad, who was coming to the end of a bad cancer. Jeffrey's parents were also in precarious health and he and Sophie went on regular trips to visit them in New Jersey.

"Who the hell is going to take care of us when we get to that age?"

This was Michael. He's ten years older than me, and I'm about the same amount older than Joe and Teresa. So there's a big age spread in this group.

"Our kids have got their own lives. Some of them are just getting started. I don't want my kid to have to worry about me like that."

"We could take care of each other," suggested JoJo, puffing away on her stogie. "We could get a big place with a central kitchen and kind of keep an eye on each other."

"Sounds like a party," said Bruce.

"Yeah, and the minute somebody gets too old and troublesome, we'll just toss him into the soup. Just kind of keep it simmering along." This was Joe, of course.

"I love this idea," said Mayes, wistfully. "We could all take care of each other."

"We wouldn't starve to death, that's for sure," said Bruno. "There's a lot of good cooks in this bunch."

"I could play the piano," offered Jill.

"I'll do the garden," said Sophie.

"I can do magic tricks," added Joe.

"I think this is a seriously good idea," said Jim. "Maybe we could find a compound—you know, with separate little cottages—and then have public areas: the kitchen, like JoJo said, maybe a big studio that the painters can all share."

"A *borgo*," said Bruno. "There are some *borgos* around that we could look at."

A *borgo* is a collection of houses—like a little village, except that there are no shops or restaurants—and occasionally

one comes up for sale. Often they're owned by many generations of a large family, and this can make the sale extremely
complicated, but it can be done.

"I don't know if I'm ready to give up my privacy," said
Jeffrey, but everybody shouted him down and told him to get
a grappa.

"What do you need privacy for? You have nothing to hide,"
said Michael.

"We'll wear blindfolds, so we can't see you," laughed
Mayes.

"And you can have your own bathroom. Is that what you're
worried about?" Joe again.

At this point Jeffrey was sorry he had brought it up and
took the advice about getting a grappa.

"Wait a minute," yelled Michael. "Who are we talking
about here? We have what? Two photographers . . ."

"Three," Teresa reminded him.

"Three photographers. Even worse. We have . . . how many
painters? We have movie designers; we have—God help us—
actors. Forgive me, Michael and Jill, but actors! We have a poet.
We have a fucking poet!"

Jim took a bow, to great applause.

"There's nobody in this group who can change a lightbulb!
We'd all be dead in three weeks. They'll find us all piled up
on each other, dead from trying to open a bag of Fritos."

"No, Bruce can do all that stuff. He's very handy. And our
kids'll help us out."

"No," said Michael, adamantly. "I don't want my kid to have
to . . ."

"No," said JoJo. "They'll do it because it's fun. Because we
are so goddamned much fun."

"Jeffrey's good at that stuff," piped up Sophie.

"Yeah, but he wants his privacy," said Michael.

"Oh, fuck you."

"Guys, guys!" said Bruno. "We haven't even started living with each other and we're having our first fight."

"What about a Ping-Pong table?" I asked.

"Oooooh." Everybody liked that idea.

"Or a pool table. I'm a good pool shooter." This was Carol, Michael's wife.

"I think Ping-Pong," I said, defending my original idea. "It's more aerobic."

At that point, more grappa was poured. Or so I was told the next day.

# TWELVE

# Two Old Broads

THE EXPAT COMMUNITY IN OUR PART OF UMBRIA—the crowd that we were fast becoming a part of—can be traced in one way or another back to the Spoleto festival. In the late 1960s, Ellen Stewart brought her La MaMa troupe to the festival and liked the town so much she bought an apartment. Bruce was in that company and a few years later, he and JoJo brought their son Miles over, put him in an Italian school, and restarted their lives. Eventually they served as a magnet, drawing some show business types—including, eventually, us—to the area.

Another strand traces back to the minimalist painter Sol LeWitt, who first came to Spoleto in the 1970s at the invitation of his Italian agent. He went to the festival for the music and he, too, fell in love and bought a house. He was the magnet that attracted many of the painters—Michael, Jeffrey, and others.

Another strand traces back to Ann Wood, who as a young woman met and married Afranio Metelli. Afranio is a painter who was born just up the road from us in Pissignano. He then had a career that took him to New York, Mexico City, and

Vallauris in the south of France where he hung out—and showed—with Picasso. After he and Ann were married they returned to Umbria, where they've been ever since. Ann was the first of a number of formidable young American women in our crowd who met and married Italian artists of one kind or another and plunged themselves into the expatriate life.

These separate artistic strands soon found each other, the bond being the Umbrian good life. They gathered into a loose aggregate, which came together over the years into a disorganized cluster until it ultimately blossomed into the crowd it is today. It's changed some over the years; new blood, like Jill and me, have come in and some of the old gang—for reasons having to do with careers, divorce, or death—are no longer there. But the strands are still deeply woven into art, the commitment to the good life is as strong as ever, and—although no one would say this out loud—it's quite like a family.

We had never met Ellen Stewart—La MaMa herself, the original strand of strands—so we managed to wangle ourselves an invitation to a big party she was having at the La MaMa artists' residence outside Spoleto. Bruce and JoJo would be there, of course. And Sophie and Jeffrey, who—although they are most definitely from Sol LeWitt's strand—were neighbors of Ellen Stewart when they first came to Umbria more than twenty years ago and are still good friends. And Mariane and George were there. George has been on La MaMa's board of directors since the early 1980s, and one of the buildings in the artists' residence is named after him.

The evening was to celebrate the graduation of the artists who had been in residence for seven weeks of the summer. It was a grand buffet with speeches and prizes afterward. Jeffrey and Sophie took us on a tour of the property, the highlight of which was a visit to Ellen's apartment there. It was like walking into a Turkish bazaar, with rugs and fabrics of every conceivable color and pattern covering the walls and floors; the room, like its occupant, is an explosion of energy, creativity, and style.

Ellen Stewart was born in 1920, or thereabouts—no one is quite certain of the date, but it makes her just about the same age as Jill's mom. In the few months preceding our meeting that night she had mounted theater productions in New York, Venice, Guatemala, and Greece—all in different languages. She's bound to a wheelchair these days but she's not bound by much else.

She started her career as a designer, in the 1950s. She got a job at Saks Fifth Avenue snipping the threads off brassieres, and within three months—or so the story goes—she was moved up to the position of executive designer of sportswear. When she decided to open her own design business, she found a basement flat for it in the East Village. A friend of hers, a playwright, convinced her that the space would also work as a theater. La MaMa—as well as New York's off-off Broadway—was born. Some two thousand productions later—productions that include the original *Hair,* which changed American theater forever—La MaMa is still going strong with Ellen at the helm, sometimes writing, sometimes designing, sometimes producing, and always inspiring.

Bruce and JoJo took us to meet her. She was in her wheelchair, sitting under a shade tree. Jill said how much she liked Ellen's bedroom, and Ellen laughed and talked about how hard it is to find anything in there.

"Nice of you to come," she told us. "Nice to have you here; don't make yourselves strangers." Then she turned to Bruce.

"Where's your oboe, honey?"

Bruce laughed. "It's sitting at home by my bed, Mama."

"That's good, honey. Keep it ready. You never know."

Afterward Bruce told us the story.

"Last year—out of the blue—Ellen called me to be in a show she was doing. I hadn't been acting—or playing the oboe—for years. She was writing, directing, and composing a show about an Italian fairy tale—operatic stuff—and she decided she needed an oboe. I pointed out to her I hadn't played in years.

"'Well, you better start practicing, baby,' she said.

"'Then I told her I didn't have a decent reed.'

"And she said, 'You make one, baby.'

"I reminded her that I had teaching obligations and I couldn't just not show up for class. But none of that mattered to her. I was going to be in her show. You can't say no to Ellen Stewart."

Mama, as everyone calls her, has a rare gift of knowing how to ask for what she wants. And she does it with such optimism and openness that she's rarely denied. Even though our meeting with her was brief, both Jill and I felt that we wanted to support the work she's doing—if only to be able to spend more time around her.

The following night—remarkably—we had dinner with Judith Malina who, with her husband, Julian Beck, had founded the Open Theater in New York in 1947. If anyone could challenge Ellen Stewart for the title of "queen of off-off Broadway," it would be Judith Malina. And we were having dinner—on successive nights—with both of them. In Umbria.

We had gotten a call from Ann Wood Metelli, telling us that her husband, Afranio, was taking part in a two-man show in a town called Cancelli. Ann asked if we'd like to come. The evening would consist of the art opening and then a poetry reading by Judith Malina, followed by dinner. I had done a film

with Judith years before and we had spent a pleasant week together on location in Brooklyn, so I was looking forward to
seeing her again.

We left the house at seven, which I thought gave us
plenty of time, but two hours later, we were still inching our
way around tight little mountain roads, trying to find Cancelli. It was much farther up the mountain than I had realized. Cancelli has a population of five, which had recently
swelled to eight. It had something to do with whether
Maurizio Cancelli was getting along with his son or not. The
Cancelli family has been in the same place since prehistory.
The story is that the apostles Peter and Paul came through
there to spread the gospel and asked hospitality of whoever
was the Cancelli of the moment. They spent the night, and in
the morning, in gratitude, they performed hands-on healing
and relieved this Cancelli of his arthritis pain.

From then on, the senior Cancelli of every generation
has had the gift of healing. The only catch is that he has to
actually inhabit the town of Cancelli; if he leaves, the power
is gone.

So Maurizio lives there. And because he's a sociable fellow, he brings the rest of the world to him—art shows, poetry
readings, dinners in the restaurant he created. Maurizio, besides his healing powers, is a painter—in fact, he was the other
painter, along with Afranio, in the two-man show.

By the time we got there, we had missed the speeches and
festivities surrounding the art show, we had missed the poetry
reading, and we were just in time for dinner. Timing is
everything. Ann met us and whisked us down to the gallery to
see the paintings, which were amazing. The theme was about
all the things that were wrong with the world—something like
that.

Then we went up to dinner and were seated at Judith Malina's table, along with her impressive entourage. It occurred to me that Ellen Stewart had been with her impressive entourage the night before. Goes with the territory. I was seated next to Judith and she didn't seem to realize that we had missed the reading, so I quickly told her how wonderful we thought it was. I reminded her of when we worked together and we reminisced a bit about that. She was very charming and I remember feeling that there was a certain sexuality about her, that she was still in the game. Not bad for a woman in her eighties. She meets your eye; she challenges you.

But confrontation is what she's known for. She and her late husband, Julian Beck—he died in 1985—challenged our ideas about everything—society, sex, politics, and especially art. They went to the barricades, they went to jail, they were the duke and duchess of the avant-garde. And the feeling I got was that she hadn't slowed down much.

On my other side was a very well-spoken fellow who worked with Judith, and he told us all about the new Open Theater season that was coming up in New York. At some point, I told him about the evening before and that we had been with Ellen Stewart.

"Isn't it extraordinary that on two successive evenings, completely coincidentally, we've had dinner with two virtual legends of the American theater?"

He sniffed and said, "Ellen Stewart is a purse designer."

Then, at a certain prearranged moment in the evening, just after the antipasto of grilled vegetables and the pasta course, Judith and her whole gang stood up, very graciously expressed their apologies—something about having to be up early the next day—and left the dining room together. Then, just seconds after the door closed behind them, waiters appeared, carrying huge trays of grilled lamb—lamb that the area is justly famous for—and started serving it to everyone else. Clearly Judith is a vegetarian and she and the entourage didn't want to make a big issue about it.

The next morning, Jill and I went to the flea market in Pissignano. It's held on the first Sunday of every month and it's the best flea market in the area. It's also a social occasion. There's only one street in Pissignano, and the market starts at one end of town and finishes at the other. There's the usual collection of junk, there are some real antiques and collectables, and parked at the lower end is a *porchetta* truck where you can buy the best pork sandwiches in the world. Ann Wood Metelli, Afranio's wife, has a table at the market where she offers jewelry, knickknacks, and such for sale, and we were standing there talking to her about our evening the night before when we saw Ellen Stewart and about ten of her gang making their way past the stalls. Ellen was being pushed in her wheelchair but she was in complete control—as always.

"Let's go get one of them pork sandwiches, honey. Before there's none left."

"Now, Mama," said one of her group, "You know your doctor told you no more pork. That's not good for you any more."

"This ain't pork, honey. This is just a *sandwich*."

And off they rolled down the street.

# THIRTEEN

# Cinema Sorci

"Would you give my mother a call, honey? She wants to talk to you."

I was in the kitchen opening a nicely chilled bottle of Grechetto, a perfect start to the happy hour, and the idea of getting on the phone with Lora wasn't making me happy.

"About her finances," she added.

"Why?" I asked, feeling the panic rise. "What did you tell her?"

I was panicky because I don't like talking on the telephone—to anyone, really. It's a cold instrument and I never feel I'm getting myself across on it. Also, I'm a very bad listener. It's a learning disorder or something. I can't hear what people are telling me at the time they say it; it comes to me later. So between my not liking to speak and my not really being able to listen, the phone is not my friend.

Besides, Lora can't hear for shit. So I have to scream everything, which is no way to communicate; it feels like bad acting. And I especially don't want to talk to her about her finances. She had been haranguing Jill for weeks about how Kathy, Ralph's daughter, was stealing her blind, and then about how she thought Alix was picking her pocket. This phone call was not going to be fun.

"I just reminded her that you said you would help her get on top of things," added Jill. "You know, get organized."

"Well, it's no big deal," I said. "She should have two accounts and get rid of everything else."

Ralph had been like Howard Hughes. He had accounts all over the place.

"She just needs a savings and a checking account," I continued. "The savings we can put in a bond account or something so it earns some money, and she'll have a checkbook for when she needs to buy something. Her mad money. And then the two accounts have to be able to communicate with each other, that's all. Just tell her . . ."

"No. You tell her." And she handed me the phone. I hate it when she does that.

"We have to get to Sophie's, don't we? I'll call her tomorrow."

We were having a screening of our documentary that night—a potluck dinner with all our friends and then Jeffrey would project our film on a big screen in his studio. Their house—when they bought it—was called Casa Sorci. So they instituted Cinema Sorci on a regular basis, showing classics, new films, and, occasionally, screenings for their friends. And they would make popcorn.

"There's time."

I grumbled and dialed the number.

"Lora? It's Mike. Your son-in-law? How ya doin', sweetheart?"

I called out to her as if she were at the other end of a football field, but all I got was silence.

"Lora?"

"I'm very angry at you."

"At me?" My voice went up an octave. Angry mothers are not my favorite thing. "Why, sweetheart? What did I do?"

"I am perfectly capable of handling my own checkbook. I paid all the bills around here until . . . well, until Ralph got sick."

"Oh, okay. I didn't know that. I have no problem with that. I didn't realize you wanted to do it. Jill told me . . ."

I tried desperately to foist it off on Jill.

"Jill's not right about everything, either, you know. I am perfectly capable of balancing my checkbook."

"Okay, Lora. That's great. Really great."

I'm shouting into the phone.

"I just thought you might want some help, you know. So . . ."

"I was in the real estate business. You didn't know that, did you? I had to deal with large transactions all the time. And you treat me like I'm a child."

"No! I think it's great that you want to do it. Look, I made a big mistake, Lora. I never should have said that. And I'm really sorry. You should take care of your money on your own. That's fine. I won't help you at all."

"There's no need to be mean about it."

"No! I mean I'll help you if you want, but . . ."

"I was the executive director of the United Fund in Green Bay, Wisconsin. Don't you think that means I must know something about money?"

"Yes, absolutely! Listen, I think you probably know a lot more than I do. Hey, you could help me with *my* finances."

There was a long silence, then, "That's not funny."

She never got my jokes.

This went on for another fifteen minutes or so and I was fighting down panic and outrage, neither of which had anything to do with Lora; it was all about my mother, who, although she's been dead and buried for eight years, still has her hooks in me pretty good. I was backtracking and tripping over myself, apologizing like an idiot, and telling Lora how impressed I was with all she's done and all she knows. I was furiously sipping down the Grechetto, which helped me keep a lid on it. But with all that, I had a strong sense that she didn't want me to back off at all. She was scared to death about her finances and didn't know what to do about them; she just didn't want to admit it. It was that appearances thing again.

Finally I got her off the phone and looked across at Jill, who was looking at me like she was a mother kangaroo, like I was a little kid who had brought home a good report card.

"What are you smiling at?"

"It just really warms my heart to see you and my mom having such a nice talk together."

And that was it. I laughed and so did she and all the tension and anger flew out the window.

"Let's go to Sophie and Jeff's," I said.

It's amazing how one woman—with a smile and a look in her eye that says *We'll get through it, baby*—can make it all better. This woman, anyway.

The movie we made—a documentary, *Emile Norman: By His Own Design*—was a big deal for us. We'd been working on it for seven years and we are, frankly, very proud of it. It's about an artist friend of ours who just turned ninety. As I've mentioned, he lives on a mountain in Big Sur, California, and his work and his life are very inspiring. We met him years before when we bought land from him in Big Sur. Then we built a house on the land and became his neighbor. Over the years we would bring friends to meet him and take them on a tour of his hand-built house and gallery, and invariably they, too, would be inspired. Sometimes their lives would change. So we felt we needed to somehow get this magic onto film.

At first we brought directors up from Los Angeles, but Emile rejected them all out of hand. In truth, he wasn't interested in doing a movie; he was too busy with his own work. This cat-and-mouse game went on for a couple of years until we met a young documentary director, Will Parinello, in Mill Valley, up in northern California. We had an instant impression that Emile would like this guy; so we hired him and a soundman for a weekend and went down to see what would happen. We had no idea whether Emile would show up well on film. We set up an interview and the moment the camera started rolling we knew it was going to work out. Emile lit up the screen; a star was born.

At that point we were thinking about making a fifteen-minute short—just to capture him for posterity. Seven and a half years later, we had an hour-long film headed for an airing on PBS. Documentaries are like that—you keep discovering things as you go along and the scope of the film keeps changing and growing. We raised money as we could, trying to keep ahead of the spending. When we couldn't raise money, we coughed it up ourselves. They say with a documentary you put in a dollar's worth of gas and go as far as that takes you, then you stop until you find another dollar's worth. That's one of the reasons it took seven years.

The screening at Sophie and Jeffrey's was the first time we had showed the film to our friends. They're all artists of one kind or another and can be very critical, so we were nervous. We needn't have been. It was a party. First was dinner, which was potluck, and in this crowd that means a real feast. Everyone cooks well, and people were pulling produce from their own gardens, so everything was fresher than fresh. And everyone brought a bottle or two of wine, of course, so by the time the screening started there wasn't a critical eye in the house.

There was a free-for-all discussion after the screening and we couldn't have gotten a better response if we had written it. After the obligatory congratulations, what people talked about was their own work—how it was changing, how they had to be braver, how they had to be true to their own vision. Emile had inspired them, and this was the reason we had set out to make the film in the first place.

Driving home, we talked about my conversation with Lora. I told Jill I thought we needed to get the power of attorney as soon as we could; then we'd set up automatic payments for her rent, telephone, and health insurance, etcetera, so that everything would run smoothly for her.

"But is she going to let us do that?"

I said I didn't know. If you listen to her words, she's definitely not going to give up control; but if you listen to the quaver in her voice, it's saying loud and clear that she's scared and needs help.

"What do you think is going to happen?" I asked.

"I don't know," Jill answered in a small voice.

"Do we move her to New York?"

"I don't know." The small voice again.

"The problem with that is she doesn't want to move. She says she loves it in Santa Barbara. All her friends are there. You can't just move somebody who doesn't want to be moved. That's kidnapping."

"Well, . . . people do it."

"They do it when the person is incapacitated. Then you have license to act in the person's behalf. But your mom's not there yet. At least I don't think she is."

"Sometimes she is."

"Yeah, true."

We thought about that a minute.

"But moving her to New York—to such a different place—could be the final blow," I said. "That could finish her. That's what happened with my mother: we moved her from her apartment because she couldn't live alone any more, and she crashed and that was that. She never recognized us again after that."

This part was true—moving someone at that age is a tricky thing. What I wasn't saying, however, was that I dreaded the idea of moving Lora to New York because of what it would do to Jill. She and her mom had a debilitating behavior pattern that went all the way back with them. It's always the same: Jill does something wonderful and successful—it could be anything from setting the table nicely for a dinner party to winning a Golden Globe award—and Lora goes to great lengths to ignore it and change the subject. It's a mean game, like a Punch and Judy show; Jill keeps setting herself up and Lora keeps knocking her down. Lora must feel in competition with Jill, and she knows she can't win, so she makes Jill disappear; she doesn't see her and doesn't hear her.

"Mommy, mommy, look what I made!"

"I just read a review of a new biography of Adlai Stevenson. I clipped it out for you."

Over and over and over. I could do with not having Lora move to New York.

"So what do we do?" Jill asked, sensing my thoughts.

I shook my head. The country road was dark and I was taking my time.

"Welcome aboard," said Jill.

"Yeah, I'm on board. Just don't hand me the phone like that any more. It makes me crazy."

"Okay. I'll do the phone."

She put her hand on my arm and let it rest there as we made our way home.

## FOURTEEN

# The Night of the Shooting Stars

WE GOT A CALL FROM WILL PARRINELLO, the director of our documentary, telling us that the film had been chosen to be a part of the IFP Market in New York. That's the Independent Film Project's yearly market, where filmmakers, television networks, and distributors—both domestic and foreign—meet, have screenings, and go to seminars. It's where the filmmakers can find not only distribution for their films, but also what's called "completion money." Getting chosen was a coup for us because—even though our film was already shot, edited, and scored, etcetera—we still needed funds to pay the royalties on all the archival footage, photos, and music that we had used to put our story into historical perspective. The rights to all this cost a fortune, so a little "completion money" would come in handy.

The only problem was that the IFP Market was happening in early September, and I had been determined to stay in Italy through the end of the month. September is an extraordinary month in Umbria. I wanted to experience the *vendemmia,* the grape harvest, in Montefalco, which is the wine center in our part of Umbria, I wanted to eat my way through the onion sagra in Canarra, and I wanted to frolic through the forest during the mushroom harvest on Monte Subasio, when the porcini come out to play. Will, our director and coproducer, understood my plight—he is, after all, Italian—and he offered to attend the IFP Market on his own. But he also pointed out that our fading celebrity could be a help in attracting attention to the film—especially in terms of PBS, HBO, Showtime, and the like, whose representatives might want to meet with us.

"I wouldn't mind, honey," said Jill in the tone she uses when she wants something. "I really wouldn't mind going back early. I could visit my mom and then we could do the IFP Market. Italy's not going away; we can come here next September."

"Or we could be dead next September."

"Oh, please, don't pull that crap on me. I hate it when you do that."

"Sorry."

"We could be dead next September if we stay in Italy, too."

"I'm . . . yeah, okay."

I brooded. In fact, I was just being pigheaded. Of course we had to attend the IFP Market; it was a great opportunity. And of course Jill wanted to go to Santa Barbara and do an on-site inspection of the situation there, which was hard to decipher over the telephone. But I thought that unless she was ready to check Lora into the dementia ward, there wasn't much to be done. The trip would be for Jill, I guess—to show up and look like she was doing something. But eventually we'd have to go home to New York and we'd be right back in the same situation—or worse, if Lora's condition continued to go south. To change things, we either had to move ourselves out to Santa Barbara, which was out of the question for a million reasons, or move Lora to New York, which had its own set of problems. It seemed to me we didn't have a good alternative.

"What about moving your mom to Italy?" I proposed, only half jokingly. "We'll set her up in the kitchen and teach her how to make ravioli."

Jill eschewed a response.

That night was the party for the Night of the Shooting Stars at Joe and Teresa's house. Jill had been working on her role of Rosalind all week and I knew she was excited about performing it. I had given Touchstone only a cursory look—just to remind myself what he was saying. This is a big difference between us—and maybe at the root of our disagreement about how much time to spend in Italy. Jill wasn't finished with acting yet. In fact, she was feeling quite in her prime, whereas I was ready to hang up the old dancing slippers. Acting has always been an odd brew for me, a measure of paralyzing anxiety before I go on, mixed with the adrenaline rush of overcoming that anxiety when I'm out onstage. It's a form of getting high, which is fine and dandy, but after a certain age there are easier ways to get high.

I've been done with acting a hundred times in my career. I tried to quit when I was in drama school, until it became clear to me I couldn't earn a living doing anything else. I got out of the business when we first got to New York and I couldn't get started; I wrote trade shows and sales meetings to pay the bills. In the 1970s, I tried the voice-over business; in the 1980s, I almost got into the restaurant business—anything to get out of acting. But somehow I kept getting lured back in, probably because there are aspects of the craft I enjoy. I'm an exhibitionist; there's no question about that. Scratch any actor and you'll come up with that particular kink. I had a teacher in drama school who said, "An actor is a person who likes to stand in the light while other people sit in the dark and watch him." I also enjoy crawling into a character's psyche and looking at things from a different point of view. You can learn a lot about yourself when you're walking around in another man's haircut.

But then there's the terror, and the older I get, the less I like to put myself into that kind of discomfort. I'll do it for money, but that's about it. When *L.A. Law* ended, my overriding emotion was, "Thank God, I never have to do that again."

Italy—buying a house there, learning a new language, becoming part of an extraordinary new group of friends, spending my days in the idle pleasures of exploring the countryside, hiking the hills, shopping at the local stores, cooking, filling the evenings with blissful indulgence—really symbolized for me my retirement from acting. When people asked me what I was doing these days—the classic question put to an out-of-work actor—I could say, "I have a house in Umbria." That seemed to take care of that.

The only problem was that I didn't quite mention my retirement to Jill. To her I said "semiretirement," which is a very fishy word. I've been semiretired since I was seventeen. An actor is either working or looking for work; in both cases, he's semiretired. But Jill was still expecting me to show up as her acting partner, and I hadn't quite come clean about the fact that I'd be happier not doing it any more.

This "partnership" evolved from 1986—thirteen years into our marriage. It was the year we became famous with the debut of *L.A. Law* at the very same moment Jill discovered she had cancer. The two events—mortality and immortality—were virtually simultaneous and our lives underwent an instant seismic shift. Previously, we had pursued our careers separately and lived our private life privately. But in 1986 we were suddenly thrust into being a publicly owned "perfect couple"—an experience that was totally weird—and we were desperately afraid we were going to lose each other. I grabbed hold of her hand and essentially didn't let it go for twenty years.

When *L.A. Law* ended, we left Los Angeles and moved north to Marin County with the thought that we would turn our attention inward, toward each other and our relationship. We took courses, together—all kinds of relationship courses, where we learned how to be even closer than we were before. We gave speeches around the country together, we did plays locally together, we created a cabaret act together, we produced the documentary together, we bought a house in Italy and started a new chapter of our life together.

And now, almost exactly twenty years after the cancer, I was gently, tentatively letting go of her hand—tentatively not because I thought she couldn't have a brilliant acting career on her own, but because I didn't want not to be touching her.

Another reason I could let the acting go was that I was writing every day. A lot of my creative juices—when I could find them—were being siphoned into writing. It's a whole new deal for me. Acting is an interpretive and collaborative art. The source material is the playwright's, the interpretation is the director's, the visual scheme is the designer's, and the manifestation of the piece comes out of a collaboration between all of them and the actors. If a production is good, it's almost impossible to tell who's responsible for what. That's why critics always get it wrong. But writing is just the writer. When I sold my last book, I had dinner with my editor because I wanted to explain to him how I was changing the whole beginning. It was going to be different from the proposal he bought and I wanted to make sure we were all on the same page, so to speak, before I got going on the book.

He looked at me as if I were crazy. "I don't have any idea how you should start. Just write the book. When you're finished, I'll read it and then I'll edit it."

Writing is uncollaborative. And I suppose I'm at a time in my life when that appeals to me.

The Night of the Shooting Stars party was in full swing when we got there. Joe had made his famous pesto with green beans. Now I know this is a digression, but if it's summertime you have to try this: Make a pesto. Buy a few handfuls of green beans, as fresh as you can find and parboil them in salted water until they're soft—that's right, soft, so that you could twirl them on a fork. Then combine the green beans with the pasta and the pesto, add a bit more pecorino and a few grinds of pepper, and dig in. It may be the most perfect summer meal of all time.

After we ate and fortified ourselves with chilled wine, we began the performance. The cast was superb. George played the Old Duke, and this was perfect casting; he is, after all, our old duke. Sophie was a fetching Celia; Jeffrey was the fusty Sir Oliver Martext; Jim, our poet in residence, was perfect as the dour Jacques; and Joe—in full drag—gave a lovely and rather touching performance as Phoebe. I went for all the cheap laughs as Touchstone and got my knuckles rapped a few times by JoJo, who played the role of producer, director, audience, and critic all wrapped up together. Opposite Jill's Rosalind was Bruce as Orlando, as gallant and handsome a suitor as one could imagine.

Jill was radiant. She deftly shed thirty years by simply opening her mouth to speak Rosalind's lines. She was forceful; she was soft. She was flirtatious; she was as true as gold. She carried herself with a regal bearing and yet you could feel the young girl's excited heart beating inside her breast. She took the night.

After the applause and the bows, George revealed a cooler filled with bottles of the best *prosecco,* which he had brought for an opening-night toast. We filled our glasses and made our way out to the backyard to watch the shooting stars—only to find that a fog had descended over the mountain and we could barely see one another's faces.

"It's okay," called out Joe. "If we drink enough *prosecco,* we'll see plenty of stars."

Why was I feeling so good? Well, the first and most obvious answer was that I had gotten through the performance and I was celebrating with a glass in my hand, which is my absolutely favorite moment in show business. But there was more to it than that. I was enjoying watching Jill shine. They say that the best male dancers are the ones who make the girl look good. The ones who try to outshine their partner may end up winning on *Dancing with the Stars,* but they're never going to score any points with her. Our partnership was still in place; it was just shifting.

## FIFTEEN

# Kiss Bidet Good-bye

THEN LORA FELL AGAIN. Frankie, who had made a habit of dropping in every morning, found her on the kitchen floor. She had blacked out, fallen to the floor, and hit her head pretty badly. Now she was in the hospital. Jill reached Lora's doctor, who was there at the hospital with her. The doctor was still unsure of why this falling was happening. She tested once again for stroke, but the result was negative. After more tests, she would move Lora first to a nursing facility until she stabilized and then back to her apartment. The doctor insisted that it wasn't necessary for Jill to come, that this was a relatively minor incident—a nasty bump on the head—and that the most important thing was to find out why she was blacking out.

Jill called Alix, who was recently back from her trip to Italy, and asked her to go and see Lora in the nursing facility. The news wasn't good. Lora was berating the nurses, occasionally taking swings at them; at one point she had to be restrained.

"I think she'll be fine once she gets back to her apartment," Alix said. "The nurse told me this is fairly common behavior after a trauma like this. I guess it just passes after a while."

Jill was frustrated because she couldn't talk to her mom —the nursing facility wasn't equipped with phones with loudspeakers.

"Does she know you?" she asked Alix.

"Oh, yeah. She keeps telling me to get her the hell out of there and back to her apartment."

"I'm coming. As soon as we can get a flight."

"Honey, don't. There's nothing you can do. By the time you get here she'll be home and she'll be herself again."

"Her doctor can talk to her. She trusts her."

"Right now she doesn't trust any doctors—even hers. She thinks the doctors killed Ralph. She keeps saying that."

"God, I wish I could talk to her. This is so frustrating. If I could talk to her I could calm her down."

"Well, they've got her on something; they're sedating her for sure."

Jill got the doctor on the phone again and asked her about Lora's mental condition. Was this Alzheimer's behavior? Swinging at the nurses? The doctor didn't think so—there were other reasons that made more sense: they had done a brain scan and found a subdural hematoma that was a result of the fall; they also found a second one that was probably from an earlier fall. Either of these could cause erratic behavior, the doctor said. Then there's something called ICU psychosis, which is common, especially in older patients, when they regain consciousness and find themselves in a hospital bed. Couple this with the stress surrounding Ralph's death and there were plenty of explanations for Lora's behavior. The doctor said she would keep a close eye on it and keep Jill apprised.

Jill called Alison and asked her to drive up to Santa Barbara so that she could be there when Lora got back to her apartment. Jill wanted to make sure there was a familiar face to welcome her. The next day Alison called and I answered the phone in the little office space we have under the stairs. I called to Jill in the kitchen to pick up the extension.

"Okay, mom. You owe me big."

"Why?" asked Jill. "What happened?"

"Well, you've got one crazy little mother there."

"It's called ICU psychosis. The doctor said it'll go away. It's from the fall and waking up in the hospital and being disoriented."

"Yeah . . . Hmm. How do I tell you this? She . . . okay, she thinks they've been doing Nazi experiments on her. They kidnapped her and took her to a secret place and drilled a hole in her brain. And the bandage on her head proves it. She's been going around telling Frankie and Tap and lots of other people to be careful—that they're next. It's a plot against old people. She's absolutely convinced that's how Ralph died."

"Nazis?" I asked.

"Well, she didn't say Nazis. That was me."

"Is there any chance that she's right?" I asked. "Is it possible that there are Nazis drilling a hole in her brain?"

"Gee," said Alison. "I hadn't thought of that."

"Guys," said Jill with real tension in her voice. "Please don't do that now. Please don't make jokes."

We both apologized. Alison and I have a history of bantering with each other. It's a way to break the father-daughter tension between us, a feeble attempt at intimacy. Jill hates it.

"We know she has a tendency to paranoia sometimes . . ."

"Mom, okay. Like this is just straight, okay? No jokes. I said to her—like you talk to a kid—I said, Grandma, remember you had a fall and you bumped your head and that's why you have that bandage."

"Yeah?"

"She came at me like a crazy woman. Her voice was like what's-her-name in *The Exorcist*. She hissed at me and told me I was like all the rest of them, that I didn't know anything, that they were coming to get the old people. Mom? She's fucked up."

After we hung up, Jill and I sat under the pergola. She looked at me and shook her head.

"She's punching people."

"I'll change the flight. We'll go and you'll calm her down."

"I'm scared of her, too, when she gets like that."

"You've seen her do that before? Like a bag lady? That's so weird. If anything, I always found her too controlled."

"When my dad left she was like that. I'm feeling it in my body right now; I'm feeling panic right now. Like when I was fifteen."

"We'll go," I said. "This is no fun anymore."

She looked at me as if I were a little puppy dog. "Are you okay? You're not going to get your September."

"Come on, honey, give me a little credit here. I'm not a total fucking idiot. There'll be other Septembers."

She nodded. "Italy won't go away."

"No. It won't go away."

"And our friends will always be here."

"Yes, our friends won't go away."

"And we'll come back when we can."

"Yep."

She took my hand over the table. Hers was still shaking.

"However, I will miss a lot of chances to eat pasta," I said. "A whole month's worth of spaghetti with pesto and green beans—gone forever."

She smiled. Thank God I could still make her smile.

"They do have all that stuff in the states, you know. They have spaghetti and green beans and basil and pine nuts."

I nodded. And then we both shook our heads. Not the same. No way.

The next day was Sunday and I spent the morning on the phone with the airlines. It was the high season and there weren't many possibilities to change the flights, but finally I got us on something six days later that connected a few times—first in Madrid, then in Atlanta, and finally to New York. From there we could get a flight to California. We needed the six days—at least—to get everything organized, to close the house, and to clear our ridiculous social calendar.

By the time I finished getting that all settled, we found ourselves—as we always do on Sundays—without a reservation for lunch. Sunday lunch is the busiest meal of the week, and we always forget that. I called Bruno to see if he had plans to go somewhere and whether we could piggyback on his reservation. Bruno is the king of Sunday lunch. He finds out-of-the-way places, little family *osterias* up in the mountains or trattorias in tiny hamlets deep in the Valnerina, which is the wild, mountainous valley to the east of us. Bruno has a nose for these places.

"Yeah, we're going to a place I found in Triponzo. Let's meet at the Fonti at twelve-thirty and you can follow us."

Our meeting place was the Fonti del Clitunno, which is a local tourist destination. It's the source of the Clitunno River and there's a park with swans. People have been coming to see it for centuries—there's a quotation from Pliny the Elder, who wrote about its tranquil beauty. For us, it's a very convenient meeting place right on the Flaminia. It has a big parking lot and a bar where you can grab a "slammer," as

JoJo calls it—a quick double espresso—just in case you're not quite fully awake.

Bruno and Mayes arrived at the Fonti with Bruno's mom, Silvana, in the backseat. Silvana lives in Rome and often comes to visit. She, too, is getting on in years and lives alone in the house where she raised her family. Bruno and Mayes have tried to persuade her to move in with them—or at least live near them—but Silvana loves her life in Rome. She plays cards regularly with her friends in the neighborhood, and Bruno's sister is nearby to keep a close eye on her. When their car pulled up, we gave them each a kiss on both cheeks and then got back in our car and fell in behind Bruno and drove to the Valnerina.

Triponzo is a one-stop-sign town on the road just past the turnoff for Norcia. There are a few houses and shops and a nondescript storefront *ristorante*—which looks a bit like a coffee shop—with a bar on the other side. It's called Il Tartufaro, which means the truffle expert, or the truffle guy. I think maybe it's a pun on *tuttofare,* which means handyman. Guerino, the owner, chef, and waiter—*il tartufaro* himself— is a friend of Bruno and he's famous as a man who knows the local mountains. He has his own herd of sheep in the hills and he forages every morning for wild greens, mushrooms, and truffles. He hunts for boar when the season is right and his pasta with a wild boar *ragù* is a specialty of the house. He also makes his own very fine red wine vinegar and will sell you some if he likes you.

We all had the boar pasta and then some grilled lamb— culled from the herd, no doubt—covered with grated black truffles, and then various plates of wild chicory, mixed lettuces, tomatoes, sautéed wild mushrooms, and some fried potatoes. Guerino hovered around us, checking to see if we fully appreciated the freshness of each ingredient.

"I can't believe you guys won't be here for the wine harvest," said Bruno, cleaning the last bits of lamb off the bone. "That's all you've been talking about."

"We've got to go back and check on my mom, Bruno," said Jill. "I think she's really losing it."

"So is mine," answered Bruno, looking affectionately across the table at Silvana, who understands no English. "But that doesn't mean I have to miss the *vendemmia*."

"Bruno!" Mayes shot him a disapproving look and Bruno laughed.

"Hey, you have to do what you have to do. When do you guys leave?"

"Next Friday."

"Oh, wow. You'll miss the whole September."

"Bruno," interrupted Jill. "Don't start. He's having a hard enough time as it is."

"No, I'm fine," I insisted. "Like Bruno said, this is what we have to do right now. When we get your mom straightened out, we'll come back. Maybe in November for the olive harvest."

We decided to throw ourselves a farewell party the night before we left. We reserved one of the long tables on the patio outside at the Palazzaccio and invited pretty much everybody we know who was still in town. Joe and Teresa had already left to be back in time to get their kids into school; Carol was going back around the same time we were because she teaches photography at Long Island University and had to gear up for that. Michael would join her a few weeks later. Bruce and JoJo would be leaving for Vietnam, where they were going to spend a year living on the proceeds of the rental of their

Umbrian house. The rest of our gang—some expats, some Italians—lived in Umbria year-round and watched us all come and go like migratory birds. We eyed one another—the ones staying and the ones leaving—each with a bit of envy for the others.

The Palazzaccio, as I mentioned earlier, is a family operation. Mamma's in the kitchen, along with Nicla, one of the daughters; the other two daughters, Danila and Teresa, run the operation out front. The older grandchildren help out by waiting on tables when they're not in school and the younger ones are often sitting at a table in the corner doing their homework or chasing the kittens around the patio outside.

We all knew this family very well. They had become like our family. Danila and her daughter, Flavia, had come to New York the year before, staying alternately at Joe and Teresa's apartment, then at Michael and Carol's. Danila was overwhelmed by New York and refused to leave the apartment for the first few days, holing up in Joe's kitchen making ravioli like a crazy woman. Then we took them all down to Chinatown and that broke the ice. They ate noodles, of course.

By the end of our farewell dinner, the two families—the expat crowd at the table and the Palazzaccio family serving us—merged over dessert and grappa. Danila and her husband, Vezio, were sitting at the table at this point, each deeply involved in conversation; Teresa stood by, making sure everyone's glass was full, but she, too, was part of the party. It was more like being in their home than at their restaurant; they were our friends, our family.

I thought about our own family—Lora was in Santa Barbara, Alison in Los Angeles, and Max in New York; Jill and I were flying all over the place—and I thought how different we were from the Italians. We loved each other, sure.

We weren't estranged in any way. But we were separate, individuated; we'd lost touch. Or rather we had lost the touch of each other, the actual, physical touch of family.

It's the American way. We take pride in the fact that our children are on their own career path and creating their own family; we take pride when they're able to have their own home with their own circle of friends. In America, an adult child who lives at home and socializes primarily with parents and family is considered odd or, at least, socially unsuccessful.

In Italy—especially in the countryside—it's quite the opposite. If a child has moved out of the house before the age of thirty-five, Mamma has some explaining to do. The kids are often in the family business and they socialize—not exclusively, but often—in the family circle. Perhaps the difference is economic. In Italy, young people starting out are not well paid, whereas the older people have very good pensions and usually own their houses. So it makes sense for the children to live at home while they're getting started. It's not unlike America a generation or two ago, when the nation was coming out of the Depression and families had to stick together for their very survival. But these days in America it seems that the sooner the younger generation can be off on their own, the better. They've gained a lot more independence than their Italian counterparts but they've also lost something in the trade-off.

# SIXTEEN

# Money

WE DECIDED TO STOP FOR TWO NIGHTS in New York before heading out to check on Lora. We needed to reorganize, pay some bills, and check in with our agents to remind them we were still alive. Joe and Teresa had us over for an easy dinner on the evening we arrived. This is another tradition with us—a very sane one. Those who have been traveling get a home-cooked meal on their return. We call it the soft landing dinner.

"Just drop your bags and come on over. I'm making a spaghetti carbonara and Teresa's doing a big salad. Simple, simple."

We gave them the most recent news of everyone in Umbria and described in detail what we had to eat the night before at the Palazzaccio. It felt a bit as though we hadn't left Italy yet, and that was nice for all of us.

The next day we had a meeting with our attorney, and when we told him why we were going back to Santa Barbara, he stressed the importance of getting Lora to sign a power of attorney for Jill while she was still able to do so. He said if we waited and Lora became incapable, whatever money she had could be tied up for years. He gave us all the forms we needed and wished us luck in what he thought might be a delicate negotiation.

The real problem wasn't the money—there wasn't that much of it, anyway—but rather what the money symbolized: control. Who would call the shots? When Lora signs the power of attorney, does that mean she's handing over to Jill—and by extension, to me—control over her life? Do we then decide where she lives and in what kind of facility? Or does she decide? At what age and mental condition can you just brush a person aside and take over the reins? There were times when Lora was completely competent, and then there were times when she wasn't. Sure, she had episodes of paranoia, belligerence to the nurses, and memory loss; but she still spoke in full sentences and had strong, cogent opinions. Weren't we obligated to consider them? In her mind, she certainly wasn't ready to abdicate control. And if we ended up in a wrestling match, we'd lose her trust forever.

Also, if we did make the decisions, we weren't at all sure we'd make the right ones. Should we encourage her to move into Elmview—the dementia ward? It was a beautiful facility, designed and furnished in a style similar to her apartment; there were people there she knew; she could have her own furnishings and art in her room; and her friends would be near. All those things were positive—except for the friends, who could go either way: Lora might feel stigmatized by having her peers see her in the dementia ward; she might actually prefer to go to someplace farther away from the people she knew. Should we try to find someone to live with her as a kind of roommate and caretaker? Or there might be some guy around who'd want to cuddle up with her.

Then there was the issue of Jill and me: what was best for our life? Again, tricky. Jill didn't admit it, but she hesitated to bring up the idea of moving Lora to New York because she was sure I'd be dead set against it. She was right, of course. I was afraid it would curtail our lifestyle, hem us in. It's not that this hadn't come up before—the idea of Lora in New York. I actually broached it as a possibility on a number of occasions, just to show what a good guy I was. But with body language I made it quite clear to Jill that I didn't really mean it, and she was hesitant to push the issue. So it just hung there between us like a bad smell in the room that everyone decided to ignore.

When we got to Santa Barbara, the reception was icy. Lora wouldn't look at Jill when we first got to the apartment. And I was clearly on the shit list. Lora looked off into the distance and refused to acknowledge that we were standing there.

"Mom?"

No answer.

"Mom, look at me."

Lora tilted her chin up a little higher.

"Mom, you know I love you. You know I want what's best for you, don't you?"

I excused myself and went outside. I thought maybe I was an impediment to progress, since Lora had me pegged as the guy who was stealing her money. After about fifteen minutes I came back and they were at least looking at each other and talking. Jill was kneeling on the floor in front of Lora's chair, holding her hand. Lora looked at me warily.

"Hi, honey," I said.

"Well, there's nothing I can do, is there? You hold the cards."

"No, Lora, that's not the way it is, at all. We just want to help you do whatever it is you want to do. We're your family."

"Uh-huh," she said, implying that she didn't believe me for a second. "If you want to help me, give me back my money. I have no money. You've taken it all. Look in my wallet; there's nothing."

"Of course you have money," I said, stumbling over myself to grab her checkbook. "Look, you have a lot of money in here. And a lot more in those other accounts Ralph set up. We're going to help you put it all together in one place so you can see what you have. I mean, if you want us to."

"And if you need cash in your wallet, all you have to do is go downstairs to Josie and she'll give it to you," said Jill.

"I'm not asking her for money. Why should I have to beg for money?"

"No, it's your money," insisted Jill. "That's just the system they have here for people who don't drive and can't get to the bank easily. Ralph used to do it all the time. They just bill your account at the end of the month."

"I'm not begging for my own money."

"It's not . . . okay, mom, we'll find another way."

This was the first of a series of dramatic scenes we played that week over her money. Each time, Jill knelt in front of her mother and begged her to admit that we were not thieves. The power of attorney was, of course, the most delicate negotiation of all. Lora clearly understood its significance, that it would legalize what she most feared—the ceding of control over her life.

Jill got on her knees, took Lora's hand and started her pitch. The repetitiveness of the litany had a soothing, almost hypnotic effect.

"Mom, you know I want what's best for you, don't you?"

"Well . . ." Lora shook her head, indicating that she didn't know anything of the kind.

"Mom, look at me. It's Jill, Mom."

"I know who you are."

"And do you think I want to hurt you? Do you really think that?"

Lora smiled sardonically.

"I love you, Mom. And I want to help you. Mike, too. He just wants to help you have the best life you can have."

"Why would I sign that paper? I know what it says. It says you can take all my money."

"It's not for now, Mom. It's in case you get debilitated in some way; if you fall again and have to go to the hospital, then I'll be able to help you, that's all. It's just in case. Ralph did it."

"He never did."

"Mom, Ralph signed it for Kathy. So that she could pay your bills. Ralph wanted to make sure you were safe and that your money was safe. He was a great guy and he loved you and he wanted you to be safe."

"Ralph would never sign a thing like that."

"He did, Mom. To make you safe."


Once she signed the power of attorney and another form that gave Jill the power to make medical decisions for her, we moved on to the Jesse James part of the trip, the three of us driving around Santa Barbara from bank to bank, closing accounts. And each time—at each bank—when the moment came for Lora's signature, we held our breath as she read and reread the document, sighing and shaking her head. At the last bank, the manager told us that we couldn't close the account until we emptied a safe-deposit box that was under Ralph's name. To do that we had to get Ralph's death certificate, their marriage license, and various pieces of Lora's identification. Then we scoured the apartment and all of Ralph's files for the key to the box. Nowhere. We called Kathy, who knew nothing about it. Why, she asked, did he have a safe-deposit box?

Finally, the bank hired a guy to drill open the box. We sat there in a small office in the bank while he drilled away. I tried to make jokes about what we might find in there, all of which went completely unappreciated. Lora was nervous, convinced there would be some kind of evidence that would expose Ralph's secret sex life. The box was empty, of course.

As the week passed, Lora became less afraid. Jill's presence eventually did calm her, and she was more her old self. We had some nice dinners with her friends at the retirement community; we took her out to a restaurant one night and actually managed to talk about things other than her money. We told her all about our upcoming week in New York at the IFP Market and how excited we were about screening our movie in public for the first time. She remembered Emile, the subject of the film, and she seemed excited for us about the screening. At one point, we gently broached the possibility of her helping out at the dementia ward, but she saw through that instantly. She would have none of it.

On the morning of our departure, we went over to have breakfast with her and found an emergency at her apartment. The nurse from the clinic downstairs had brought Lora's morning medication and found her passed out on the bathroom floor. She called an ambulance, which was on its way. Lora's friend Meg was there, as were Frankie and Tap. We called Lora's doctor and she said she would be there to meet us at the hospital.

I canceled our flight—I was getting to be quite an expert at that—and changed it to the following day, just in case.

Depending on Lora's situation, we could still get back to New York for the opening session of the IFP Market.

After a full morning of tests, the doctor had a breakthrough. She discovered that Lora had something called Tachy-Brady syndrome, which sometimes left her without enough blood flowing to her heart. That's what had been causing the blackouts. The doctor immediately ordered a pacemaker to be implanted, and she felt that this would bring an end to the falling. Then she put Lora on a drug that would relieve her anxiety.

The next morning Alix, the doctor, Jill, and I had a meeting at Lora's bedside. Jill was able to get the hearing aid in so that Lora could at least hear the discussion, if not actually participate. Jill explained to her about the pacemaker, and that seemed to make her feel better; it finally explained why she had been falling and held out the hope that it wouldn't happen again. It was odd to see her sedated; she slurred her words a bit and her eyes weren't as focused, but at least she wasn't punching any nurses. We decided to follow the same procedure as we had the last time Lora was in the hospital—she would go to the nursing facility for a day or two, Alix would look in on her, then she'd go back to her apartment when she was able to get around on her own. But there would be one difference: now she wouldn't be blacking out.

Jill and I caught the flight back to New York and that night attended the opening cocktail party of the IFP Market. It was a fun party, filled with bright, young filmmakers, drinking and holding forth. We were a little dazed. We felt a bit as if we were at that other famous party—that one on the *Titanic* just before it hit the ice.

# SEVENTEEN

# Scenes from the IFP

THE ANGELIKA FILM CENTER sits on the block between Mercer and Broadway on Houston Street, which divides the East Village from Soho. That also puts it right around the corner from New York University. The Angelika is a neighborhood movie palace that, since 1989, has been the place to see what's new in independent, foreign, and cult films. And every year, for one week in September, it closes to the public and serves as the screening venue for the IFP Market. The Angelika's theaters and screening rooms are all belowground, accessed by a long escalator, but the lobby—complete with café and popcorn stand—is on the street level. It's light and spacious and the perfect place for all the socializing and general schmoozing that takes place during the IFP Market.

Jill and I were almost certainly the oldest filmmakers at the IFP—by forty years in some cases—but that turned out to be fun, hanging out with the young people. They're from a different planet, these budding filmmakers. Sure, they've heard about failure and rejection, but they haven't yet had the actual, physical experience, so they're heedless, and totally testosterone-driven. The buzz in the lobby was palpable.

They treated Jill and me like the old sages that we are, even though most of them had a lot more experience in filmmaking than we did—they had all done student films, at least, whereas most of our past work had been on the other side of the camera. They had a lot to teach us. And after the week we had just spent in Santa Barbara, getting to hang out with the kids in the lobby of the Angelika was like coming up for air.

Jill was doing double duty. Between screenings, meetings and seminars, she was on the phone regularly with Santa Barbara. Alix told her that Lora had to be restrained again because she was attacking the nurses both verbally and physically. Jill tried to talk her mom down on the phone, to calm her and assure her that she needed to listen to the nurses, but without the special telephone it was hopeless. The doctor told Jill that Lora could go home the following day if she could be stabilized. Whatever she had been given to calm her down seemed to be having the opposite effect, until finally the doctor took her off that medication and tried another.

The next day was also our big screening, our world premiere, if you will. Although it wasn't officially open to the public, we had some friends and family coming, as well as our editor, Mary Lampson; our associate producer, Sue Kim; and our publicist, Judy Katz—all of whom are based in New York. Will, our director and coproducer, was in from California, and he helped organize everything to make sure we got a sizable audience from the people attending the IFP Market—other filmmakers as well as distributors, television executives, film festival directors, anyone who might be interested in marketing the film. We met a woman at a seminar who has a company, based in San Francisco, that specializes in acquiring rights for music, photographs, and archival footage. Because this was the next big step we had to take with the film—getting the rights and finding a way to pay for them—we had a number of meetings with her. We also interviewed people from various insurance companies that specialize in what's called "errors and omissions" insurance, which protects the filmmakers and anyone who airs or distributes the film from any kind of lawsuit. Between all these meetings, we attended other screenings and got to know the filmmakers afterward.

That evening on the phone, Jill arranged to hire a private nurse to accompany Lora back home the following day and stay with her around the clock until we were able to fly out there after our week at the IFP Market. Then we'd try to figure out what the hell to do next. We knew from past experience that Lora wasn't going to be happy with having a person living in, but it seemed to be the only way—at least until she calmed down and was herself again.

The next morning, around eleven o'clock New York time, Jill got a frantic call from Alix, saying that the retirement community people were not going to let Lora back into her apartment. They had a rule that people in assisted living could not have twenty-four-hour aides. They also said they wouldn't let her back in without an aide, because the last time she came home from the hospital she had been belligerent and "upsetting to the other residents." So she couldn't go home with an aide and she couldn't go home without one. Jill panicked— Lora was paying quite a bit of money every month for her apartment, and now they wouldn't let her live in it. She called Josie at the assisted-care office, but Josie had left for vacation the day before. Then Jill called the director of the community, for whom we had done some fund-raising—Jill thought he would use his muscle to let Lora go back home. He was out of town as well. The only person with any kind of power was the head nurse at the assisted-care clinic.

"What's going on there?" Jill asked the head nurse. "Why can't my mother go home? This is ridiculous."

She listened for a moment and her face reddened. "What rule? You have a rule that says people can't live in their own apartment?"

"That they're paying quite a bit of money for," I added from the cheering section.

"That's insane!"

She listened again.

"I know you've got a rule—you told me." Her voice was rising. "But you're going to have to break your fucking rule this time, because my mother needs to go home. To be in her own apartment, with her own furniture, and her pictures . . ." Now she was crying.

"What's your name? You are not a nice person and I'm going to speak to someone about you."

Jill hung up. She told me later that it felt as though a knife had gone through her heart.


The screening started at one o'clock. It was held in one of the larger theaters downstairs at the Angelika and it was jam-packed. Will had been working with the tech people to make sure there would be no glitches with the picture and sound. Then he, Jill, and I went to the front of the audience and made a little welcoming speech; as the lights went down and the screening began, I sneaked out to the lobby to get a bag of popcorn because, well, a movie isn't a movie without popcorn.

The film starts with a long shot of Emile—working away in the middle of the night. We see him from far away through the window of his studio, the only light in a pitch-black night. The camera slowly pushes in as we watch him sanding an almost finished inlaid wood sculpture. J. Michael Friedman's eloquent music—piano and cello—evokes mystery and a touch of melancholy. I reached over and took Jill's hand and gave it a squeeze. We had been working on this movie for almost eight years. She looked over at me with the saddest smile I've ever seen. Now, it said, we've got another job to do that will be no less consuming.

The reaction to the screening was thrilling, beyond our expectations. We had been attending many of the other screenings, and there was no question that our film was farther along in the process than most of the others. Many of the films had been edited by the director, and this procedure makes sense if you have to save money. But the fact that we had Mary Lampson, who is one of best editors in the documentary world, put our film in another category. At least we thought so. The day before, we had met with some people from various PBS series—*American Masters, Independent Lens,* and *P.O.V.*—as well as executives from PBS itself. Some of them made it to the screening and gave us a very enthusiastic response. They felt—as we did—that PBS would be a perfect place for our film.

That night we had dinner with Max, which is always a treat for us. Even though we live in the same city, it's hard for us to get onto his social calendar. First of all, he lives on vampire time—he's up all night, playing and partying, and then sleeps until the afternoon. He was in three bands at the time, two of which—playing rock-funk music—had regular gigs in New York; the other was a small jazz combo that he did for love. Then there was his church band—the gospel trombone choir—that played every Sunday at the church in Harlem and often went out on tour. Plus, all of these groups take time to rehearse when they're not gigging. He's a busy boy.

But he's never too busy to be tempted into a steak dinner with his parents. Will, our director, joined us and we went to the little place upstairs at the Fairway Market on Broadway. It's a burger joint in the afternoon and a steak house at night. The meat is the same great aged prime that you can buy downstairs at the market, and this place knows how to do it right. We told Max about the screening that day and how exciting it was, and he caught us up on his whirlwind life. Then he asked about his grandma.

"It's not good, honey," said Jill. She took a deep breath and let it go.

"Why? Is she sad about Ralph?"

"She's . . . she just losing it. And they won't let her back into her apartment."

"What?"

"They . . . have a rule or something that she can't live in her apartment with a full-time aide and she needs one right now, so she has to stay in the skilled nursing center and she hates it. And she's beating up the nurses, and . . ."

Max laughed and shook his head. "She's beating up the nurses? My little grandma?"

"I wish it was funny. I don't know what to do, Maxie. I don't know what's best to do."

"You have to move her to New York, Mom."

Jill looked across the table at me; there was the briefest pause and then I nodded. And that was it. Out of the mouths of babes. Not that we hadn't thought about it before, not that we hadn't discussed it to death already; but the simple, unequivocal statement from Max sounded so right when he said it that there didn't seem to be any other way to think about it.

"We're her family," added Max, as if that was all there was to be said about it.

After dinner we were walking up Broadway. I was talking to Will, and Jill and Max were up ahead of us. They had their arms around each other.

When we got back to our apartment, our heads were spinning. Okay. We'll move her to New York. But to where? Our apartment is way too small. We have a second bedroom that we use as an office: it has a folding couch, but when you open it, there's no room to sit at the desk. No, no way. Too tight, too close.

I went online and looked for places near us—assisted-care facilities, nursing homes, places that catered to Alzheimer's patients. That was the problem; we didn't know exactly where Lora was in terms of her dementia. Jill was convinced that once she got out of the hospital and back into her own environment, her erratic behavior would go away and she'd be herself again. Forgetful maybe, but herself. This meant that assisted care would be best—she'd have her own apartment, much like the one in Santa Barbara, with an aide to come in and check on her a few times a day and administer her meds. Then Lora would be free to take part in all the cultural activities in New York. Jill had an image of taking her mom to the Met and to the Museum of Natural History; they'd have lunch together, go to Central Park. Hey, New York is a perfect place for an older person—you don't need to be able to drive, everything's available night and day, and everything can be delivered. Heaven, right?

But what if Jill was wrong about this? What if Lora didn't become her old self again? Then what kind of place would she have to live in?

The next morning we had meetings at the IFP—with PBS people, with HBO, with an insurance salesman, with a distributor from Europe who thought our film might play well over there. We saw two screenings—of filmmakers we had been getting to know during the week of the IFP Market. In the afternoon we took a subway uptown to a place that billed it-self as a "senior residence." It was not far from our apartment and was supposed to be one of the better places in town. We met with some of the staff and told them our situation, and they said they thought this would be the perfect place for Lora. They had a studio apartment available and she would take all her meals down in the dining room. They had all sorts of planned activities, trips, clubs, and concerts—all made avail-able to the residents. The price was remarkably similar to what she had been paying in Santa Barbara. But, with all that, the place couldn't have been more different from Lora's spa-cious complex in Santa Barbara. This was New York City. So instead of a beautiful mountain view, Lora's apartment would look out onto a brick wall; instead of a sunny campus with lawns, she would face a crowded New York apartment lobby when she went downstairs in the morning, filled with an-nouncements about the Jewish high holy days. And once she went outside, she would have to deal with the cacophony of New York: the crowds, the smells, the traffic, the hyperkinetic energy. How would she respond to this? And there was the weather. Santa Barbara is temperate year-round—perfect for Lora's arthritis, which is why we moved her there in the first place. The New York winter would be brutal for her, and the steamy summer no better.

There was virtually nothing in this move that would be good for Lora; everything would be a step down, at least—no friends, an alien environment, a sea of strange faces, bad weather, noise, and dirt. The only thing on the positive side was that Jill was here. Her family—her only family—would look out for her.

# EIGHTEEN

# Moving Mom

ON THE PLANE RIDE TO SANTA BARBARA, Jill and I did a lot of not looking at each other, so I sat there silently projecting what was on her mind. She's probably thinking, I thought, that if she looks at me, I'll retract my nod. Which is absurd, of course. A nod isn't retractable; I may hate the idea of moving Lora to New York, but the nod stands. She's probably thinking that I got pushed into it because Max was so heroic and sure. Well, yeah, what am I supposed to say after that?

She's probably thinking that I must have a lot of guilt, because when my mother went into her dementia, I was three thousand miles away from her. And if I could have been farther, I would have been. Yes, I helped out financially, but my brother Ed did all the grunt work—moving her to assisted care and then to the nursing home, dealing with the doctors, dealing with my mother's craziness. I stayed far away on the other coast and wrote the checks. Now I'm moving Jill's mother close to us so that we can be there for her, be her family.

Jill's probably thinking that I'm worried about money, which would be correct. If Lora's expenses are the same in New York as in Santa Barbara, her money will last less than a year. And New York has to cost more. So, when her money runs out, then we'll use our money. And when our money runs out, I'll shoot myself. Because we were on television, it's hard to convince people that we have to worry about money, but it's true. We made a lot of money twenty years ago, but virtually nothing since. We have a nice retirement set up—thanks to yours truly—but Lora's expenses could quickly reduce those lovely plans to rubble. Jill never worries about money, never thinks about it.

Then, somewhere over Arizona, I finally broke down and asked her what she was thinking. She shook her head slowly and took my hand.

"I'm worried that we're doing the wrong thing, that we're making a terrible mistake and my mother will hate it in New York. And I know you're worried about the money."

Oh.

We went forward with the plan simply because there was nothing else to do. We called the nurse in Santa Barbara and told her we were coming to move Lora to New York. Of course, she immediately said it would be no problem for Lora to stay in her apartment with a twenty-four-hour aide until we got her packed up and ready to go.

"So . . . the ironclad rule?" we asked her with no lack of sarcasm.

"Oh, well, we can make an exception in a case like this. We want to make it easy for you."

Yeah, easy for us to get Lora out of there so that they can re-rent the apartment. It all comes down to real estate.

We found Lora in the skilled nursing place looking like a street person. She was restrained in the bed, her hair was disheveled, and her eyes were wild. She looked at us like it was all our fault. While I got all the paperwork taken care of, Jill helped to dress her and put her in a wheelchair, all the while talking her down.

"It's okay, Mom. We're here now. We're going to take you home with us. I'm so sorry you had to go through this, Mom. It's such a terrible place. But you fell and they took you to the hospital. We're taking you home now, Mom."

And every time Lora started ranting about being kidnapped by evil doctors, Jill soothingly reassured her that her nightmare was over and that we'd take care of her now.

Alix met us at the apartment and we started to figure out what we were going to do with all her stuff. We found a guy to buy all the furniture and we picked out some favorite art pieces, books, correspondence, and photos and arranged to have them shipped to New York. And then there were Lora's "papers"—boxes and boxes of newspaper clippings and magazine ads, pasted into albums, pressed into books—all of them meaningless.

"May 14, 1978—Orchid Show at Minneapolis Civic Center." Lora had never raised orchids and had never lived anywhere near Minneapolis, and this clipping was thirty years old. There were millions of others. She filled her life with this stuff and it was of the greatest importance to her. Jill sat with her—in a pose that was becoming iconic—Lora in a chair, her posture like a queen's, Jill sitting at her feet, soothing her.

"How about this, Mom? Do you want to save this? See? It's an invitation to the Policemen's Benevolent Society annual dinner. I think it was from when you lived in Green Bay. We could probably get rid of that, no?"

No. Not on your life. Lora shook her head regally and put the invitation onto the "save" pile. Oh, she definitely needed that. I marked "save" on each box once it was filled and carried it out to the car. There ended up being over twenty boxes. We shipped a few of them to New York—it didn't matter which ones—and I took the rest to the dump.

From the moment we got her back to the apartment, Jill started to explain that we were going to move her to New York to live near us. The first few times, Lora protested, and then Jill took another tack.

"It's for me, Mom. Please do it for me. I can't be this far away from you any more. My kids really want me to do this. Do it for me, Mom."

And Lora didn't fight it. She knew she was on the ropes and there was no way she could go it alone any more. I think she protested at first because she didn't want to be a burden—all that crap—but she knew as well as we did that it was the only way.

Jill showed her a brochure of the senior living center in New York and went on and on about how nice it was and how smart the people were who lived there.

"There are lots of college professors there, Mom. It's a real intellectual beehive. There was a guy we met the other day who taught at Columbia."

"Oh, that's very good," said Lora vaguely. We had no idea how much of this was sinking in, but Jill kept feeding her the information—brochures from the Met, pictures of the lake in Central Park, pictures of Lincoln Center.

"It's New York, Mom!"

If you can make it here, Lora, you'll make it anywhere.

We left her after dinner with her aide, who seemed very nice. At first Lora glared at her and told her to get out, but the fight was out of her at this point. Maybe it was a combination of the drugs and Jill's being there. I don't think she wanted Jill to see her ranting.

The next morning we went to take her down to breakfast and asked the aide if Lora had gotten any rest.

"No, we didn't get no sleep last night. She was up, packing her suitcase and unpacking it and folding all her things up again real nice. Then she was packing them back into her suitcase. She was a busy girl last night."

"Did she get belligerent?"

"What?"

"Did she try to hit you or anything?"

The aide smiled. "No, no, she was all sweetness and light. She's a real lady. I mean, she didn't want me to help or anything, she just shooed me away over into the other room. She didn't want to see my face at all. She had her job to do."

"So, no sleep?"

"No, she had her job to do."

Jill went into the bedroom to see how Lora was doing and she was in there for a while, so I peeked in to see what was going on. Jill was sitting on the bed and Lora was still folding things.

"Well, she's all dressed for breakfast," said Jill, with a weird smile on her face. Lora had done herself up in a very chic lacy black top and black silk pants. She had a lot of jewelry on, including a necklace of big red beads and matching earrings. She wore tons of makeup, bright red lipstick, eye shadow, the whole thing. She looked as if she were going out for a night of dining and dancing at the poshest club in town. Or like Blanche DuBois, all set to depend on the kindness of strangers.

"Wow," I said, because I couldn't think of anything else to say.

We went for breakfast in the small dining room downstairs, and Lora was, without a doubt, the belle of the ball. An elderly gentleman asked if he could join us at the table and the old horn-ball couldn't take his eyes off her. He fetched her more coffee and helped her to some extra toast—anything to show her that he was attentive and generous and certainly the most eligible man in the room to take her upstairs and make the earth move for her.

We spent the days sorting through her stuff and tying up loose ends at the retirement community. We had a few dinners in the main dining room with her friends and Lora bragged a bit about her move.

"My kids really want me to do this." And they all nodded in approval.

And in between all this, Jill kept up her mantra.

"You'll love this place, Mom. And you'll love New York. There's a Manet show at the Met—right when we get there. It's supposed to be amazing."

The trip was a trip. Lora kept looking at us, nodding and with her eyes popped wide open, as if to say, "This is good, right?" We got her down to a couple of bags—the rest, we explained, was being shipped. We put them in the trunk of the rental car along with our bags and her walker, and drove to the Santa Barbara airport. And all the while she looked at us with those big eyes and nodded like a scared kid, "This is good, right?"

We checked the bags through to New York, but we actually had to change planes in Los Angeles. We arranged with the airline to have someone meet us there with a wheelchair to make sure that everything went smoothly. We had gotten to the Santa Barbara airport way too early, so we bought some sandwiches and iced tea and set up in the lobby and had a little picnic. Finally, they called our flight.

We had to give up the walker when we got to security, so we had her between us. She could walk, but she was shaky. When we showed our boarding passes and IDs, the woman looked at Lora's passport and said it was no good—it had expired. Jill grabbed her mom's purse and found her wallet, which had her driver's license. Also expired. "I'm sorry," said the woman. "She can't go through."

"Wait a minute," I jumped in. "They may be expired, but they're perfectly valid government documents. I mean, she's not a security threat, you know what I mean?"

I was putting on all the charm.

"They're not valid if they're expired."

"Well, yeah, I get that, but I mean, look at her. This is going to be a very long day for her and believe me, she's not a terrorist or anything."

Wrong thing to say.

"If you'll just step aside, we have to board these other passengers."

They took us into a room with a couple of official-looking people and we told them what we were doing—moving Jill's mom closer to the family and all that—and then one of them, the senior guy, recognized us from *L.A. Law*. Bingo. We were in. Thank God the guy was old enough to remember the show.

Once we got through changing planes at LAX, we boarded our cross-country flight early—along with the families with small children—and put Lora in the seat between us. When the plane taxied and took off, Jill and I shared a look: New York, here we come. Lora, who lay down across the two of us and played endlessly with the corner of her blanket, looked up at me every couple of minutes—all the way across the country. *I'm putting myself in your hands,* the look said, *I hope you know what you're doing.*

*      *      *

We brought her to our apartment for that first night. When we walked into the long hallway filled with old photos of our kids, Lora looked at them for a long time, slowly making her way down the hall on her walker.

"Oh," she said with wonder in her voice. "This is home."

We opened the folding bed in the office and Jill made it up. Then we ordered Chinese food.

"This is New York, Lora," I said, leaning in to her left ear and shouting. "Everything can be delivered."

The food arrived almost before I hung up the phone. I don't how the hell they do it. It's like some Chinese guy is camped outside our apartment door, just waiting for me to decide to order *mu-shu* pork that night.

We opened the little cartons and set them out on the table. Lora was transfixed. She tasted everything and loved it. When I helped her to seconds of garlic beef with string beans, she let go the first real smile I'd seen from her in a long time. I didn't have the heart to tell her this wasn't her new home. She would see that tomorrow.

## NINETEEN

# Cruel and Unusual

IN THE MORNING WE WALKED Lora over to the senior residence for her interview. Clearly, she knew she was going to be on trial, because she was all spruced up. Jill, who had been up and down all night checking on her, said that Lora had spent the night wandering around the apartment, looking at the pictures of the kids and packing and repacking her suitcase. Neither of them had gotten any sleep.

We had chosen this senior residence center because it was close to us, but also because it was primarily for people who still had active lives and cognizant minds. There were very old people as well, sure, but mostly there was a sense of life in this place, a sense of energetic older people socializing. This fit Jill's dream—that her mom would snap out of this torpor, that she'd get her mental energy back, and that she'd have a new chapter of her life in New York.

The interview was to be conducted not by the residence, which is basically a real estate organization, but by a separate company—an agency that markets elder care. You can purchase anything from a few "look-ins" a week to full meds administration, all the way to round-the-clock care. This interview was to determine exactly how much care the agency thought Lora would need.

The entire staff of the care agency—the aides, the nurses, and the administrators—were from the Caribbean islands. Most, I think, came from Jamaica, but there were also a lot from Haiti and the Dominican Republic. This gave the place a pleasant "Don't worry, be happy" feeling. But Jill, I could see, was plenty worried. What if Lora was too far gone to be accepted at a place like this? What if the agency told us she needed to be in a nursing home instead?

When the interview started, Jill tried to coach from the sidelines, but the nurse cut her off with a look.

"Do you know where you are, Lora? What city?"

The nurse had been told about Lora's hearing problem, so she belted out the question loud and clear. Lora focused on her like a laser. She nodded her head a couple of times in the hope that a simple affirmative would be enough—yes, I know what city I'm in. But the nurse didn't buy it.

"What city, Lora?"

Lora nodded again. And then, after a long wait, she came through.

"New York. New York City." And her face had that expression that said, "See? I'm not so dumb as you think I am."

"Who's the president now, Lora?"

More nods.

Then, "Well, he's not very good, is he?"

She got high marks for that. Next question. While I was watching this grilling, I thought back to my mother again. When her Alzheimer's disease was starting to get bad, we had her at our house for a visit. It was around the time that "Trivial Pursuit" was all the rage, and we were playing it around the kitchen table. When my mother's turn came, we asked her the question—something about a song from the 1940s—and she furrowed her forehead and nodded a bit. The nod, it seems, is universal. Then she said with great conviction, "I know this." So we gave it to her. "Trivial Pursuit" on the honor system.

Lora picked up steam as her interview went forward. She had been faking her way through conversations all her life and she had it down pretty good. The answers weren't spot-on but they were close enough and vague enough to get her by. Afterward, the nurse and Jill met privately while I sat with Lora in the waiting room. I held her hand and she seemed to like that.

At one point she leaned over and said, "Well, that was pretty scary."

I squeezed her hand and realized that her mind was in better shape than I had thought. She knew where she was.

Jill came out of the office with a big smile on her face. The nurse had been very impressed with Lora and thought she needed only an aide to look in on her a few times a day and tuck her in at night, plus a nurse to administer her meds. Her mom had hit a home run. Never mind that we all knew that, at least in her present condition, Lora would need a lot more care than that. Jill knew it, I knew it, and I think the nurse knew it. But we all smiled and pretended it wasn't so. We signed a contract.

Okay. One hurdle down—she's in. Now it was time to show Lora her new living arrangement and see how she responded. Before we'd left for Santa Barbara, we had rented some nice-looking furniture for her new apartment, which we'd augment with Lora's personal things—her own art for the walls, a few small pieces of her furniture, family photos, and such— as soon as it arrived from Santa Barbara. Jill bought a beautiful orchid as a surprise to be waiting for Lora when she first walked into her new home.

But when we went to the office to finish up the paper-work the staff people told us there was a problem: the apartment that they'd promised us, the one we'd already paid the rent on, the one that had a little sunshine peeking through the window for a couple of hours a day, wouldn't be available for two more weeks. I suppose the previous tenant had lived a little longer than anyone expected. So we were going to have to put Lora in a temporary apartment, which wasn't —they said with cheesy smiles pasted on their faces—quite as nice.

As we went up in the elevator, Jill repeated over and over into Lora's hearing aid, "Mom, this is not your apartment; this is a temporary apartment, yours is going to be a lot nicer." Lora nodded and nodded.

I opened the door with the key and looked inside. It was a fucking dungeon. The shades were up, it was the middle of the day, and you couldn't see your hand in front of your face. There was no air and it smelled like mildew. I turned on the light and there was our rented furniture crammed into this much-smaller-than-expected space, and there—on the di-nette table—was Jill's orchid.

Jill went into a cold panic. No way would this work. Her mom would throw herself out the window rather than live here. She called the office and screamed at them, "We want the apartment you promised us, the apartment we paid for." There was nothing to be done.

Lora got very quiet and small. She sat on a kitchen chair and barely moved.

"Should I go get her luggage?" I asked as softly as I could. Jill shook her head.

"She can't live here, honey."

"So, what do we do?"

We both stood there in silence. We felt like bumbling idiots. We should have taken more time; we should have planned this better. But we hadn't had more time—Lora was being restrained in a hospital bed, cursing and ranting; the people in Santa Barbara wouldn't let her back into her apartment. What the hell were we going to do? Leave her tied up until we figured out a soft landing in New York?

Jill went into high gear, as she always does under stress. She started moving furniture and making the bed and turning on every lamp she could find. I wanted to disappear, as I always do under stress, and Jill read me like a book.

"Yeah. Go and get her suitcases. Then come right back. We're going to need some things."

We spent the rest of the day fixing the place up. I was the gofer, buying sheets, a bedspread, more lamps—anything that could turn this broom closet into an apartment. While I was running around, Jill was creating magic.

"So, Mom, where do think this cushion should go? It kind of goes nicely on the chair, don't you think?"

And Lora robotically pitched in, moving little things around and nodding her head.

At around five o'clock, a nurse came up with Lora's meds. Then she said an aide would come and escort Lora down to dinner.

"Oh, we'll do that," said Jill. "We'd like to do that."

"Well, the rules say we have to take her down, so someone's coming to do that. But you can come along."

We took the elevator down to the basement, following the aide. When the elevator door opened, a smell hit my nose and I felt my whole system rebel. I'm sorry to be a snob about this, but I think I'd truly rather die than have to eat food that smelled like this. The crappy institutional food at the place in Santa Barbara—food that I went to great extremes to avoid—smelled like Thomas Keller's French Laundry compared with this. This was all old, old, second-rate, criminally overcooked food.

The aide asked someone in charge where Lora's table was, and they took her over and seated her. There were a couple of extra seats, so we joined her.

"I'm sorry, but you'll have to leave her now," said a woman in charge. "We don't have room for guests in the dining room. You can visit with her after."

No way Jill was leaving. If that woman had insisted on throwing her out, Jill would have killed her, on the spot, dead. The woman got the message and gave Jill some space. I, on the other hand, couldn't get out of there fast enough.

"Go, honey," she told me. "I'll meet you at home."

Around 10:30, Jill walked through the door, looking beaten up. Lora had refused to eat the food—I thought this proved that she was still in her right mind. Jill took her out of the dining room and upstairs to the lobby area where people gathered for various activities, concerts, sing-alongs, whatever. And Lora just shut down. She went silent and wouldn't look at Jill.

"I don't know what to do when she does that. She used to go silent sometimes when I was a kid and it scared me to death. It still does."

She started to cry. "Don't you ever do that to me," she said.

"I won't, honey."

I held her. At this point, she was what? Ten years old? Six years old?

"Finally I took her upstairs and tried to help her get ready for bed. I got on my knees and begged her to talk to me, to let me know what she's feeling."

"And?"

"She said, 'You took me away from all my friends. I don't know anyone here. I'll be alone.' And I said, 'No, Mom, I'll be here.'"

"And she said, 'No you won't. You'll be busy. You'll go away. I'll be alone.' And she's right. What have we done, honey?"

We pondered that one for a while. Then I tried to get some food into her. Jill needs food when she's under stress, but she forgets. I had bought some poached salmon and some string beans at Zabar's, and I warmed them up for her. She had a little.

"Well," I offered, "the first day has got to be the worst. Maybe tomorrow will be a little better. And then the next day a little better. You know?"

The phone rang. Emergency. The nurse had come to give Lora her nighttime meds, and Lora had taken a swing at her. Then she had cursed the nurse and starting screaming racial epithets, calling her a monkey. The nurse tried to restrain her and they got into a wrestling match. The people at the center told us to come and get her. We brought her back to our apartment—this time we covered the three blocks in a taxi—and put Lora into the folding bed. She didn't sleep.

# TWENTY

# The Fall

THE NEXT MORNING, WE TOOK LORA BACK to her apartment and tried again. We met with the aide who had gone three rounds with her the night before.

"She's strong. And she's mean. I'm not going back there with her no more. I don't care what they say."

"But don't you have to deal with people like this all the time? People with Alzheimer's? Or depression?"

"No, we have very nice people here. Nobody's hitting nobody."

Jill marched down to the office to negotiate with the head nurse. I stayed up in the apartment with Lora and held her hand. This seemed to work in terms of calming her down; better than the drugs, anyway. The apartment wasn't really the problem. She seemed to understand that she'd be moving to a nicer place in a couple of weeks—although we didn't want to get her hopes up too high, because the nicer apartment wasn't really all that much nicer. The problem right now was with the aides. First of all, she couldn't hear them. So the aide may be crooning in her lilting Jamaican way, calling her darlin' or sweet thing, and telling her how she's going to help her get dressed, but not having heard any of that, Lora suddenly gets surprised by a stranger with a black face who's trying to shove her arm into a sleeve. So she hauls off and belts her.

But now she was calm. I just kept stroking her hand and that seemed to do it. I learned this hand-stroking technique with my mother, the last time I ever saw her. My brother had called me and said that I'd better come, that the nurses were putting our mother on hospice care and that this meant the end was close. Jill and I flew to Baltimore and joined my brother to meet the nurses and the doctor and to sign whatever forms were necessary. My mom at this point was like a two-year-old, chanting nonsense syllables. She had no idea who we were, but she was happy to see us; she was happy to see everybody. She was like the puppy of the fourth floor. My brother kept repeating that she wasn't our mom—that our mom had left a long time ago—and I think I felt the same way. I didn't quite know how to relate to her, and Jill suggested I hold her hand, so I did. She may not have known who I was, but I was holding her hand and stroking it gently and that made me someone she wanted to be around.

I stayed with Lora and held her hand while Jill went down to the office with the head nurse and tried to regroup. They agreed that they had drastically underestimated Lora's problems, and they needed to increase the hours of care, possibly to round-the-clock care, at least until Lora calmed down and accustomed herself to the radical change in lifestyle that we had thrust on her.

Then they got into a discussion of Lora's behavior. Jill tripped over herself trying to apologize about the racial stuff. Her mom, she explained, was an Adlai Stevenson Democrat, a staunch liberal, a lifelong defender of equal rights for all people, and now she had turned into Archie Bunker. The nurse waved that off.

"Mrs. Tucker, I've heard everything. Don't even think about it."

But Jill found herself in her old position of defending her mother, trying to explain to the world that Lora is really a much better person than people think. Now the situation was dire: if the head nurse decided that Lora couldn't be managed, the staff would throw her out of the building.

The nurse said she had an aide who was very highly thought of, and she would try this aide out with Lora and see what happened. Then she said she would talk to the in-house doctor about upping Lora's antianxiety medication. Jill agreed immediately. We had to stabilize her in this situation before we could evaluate her future here.

Thus began a parade of caregivers—or is it caretakers? Hard to tell. Of course there are wonderful people in this profession, then there are some real stinkers, and the vast majority of them are somewhere in between—just as in any other business. The aide who had been so highly touted by the head nurse turned out to be pretty good. She had experience with dementia patients and she seemed to understand how to approach Lora—and when to back off. The problem was that we had her only once or twice a week, and for short shifts. Jill begged the head nurse to limit Lora's help to the same one or two people every day—so that Lora could get used to them and finally accept them. But the nurse told her that the company doesn't work that way. It has to shuttle numerous aides in and out—so that the whole staff is involved with the "client." She put that out as a plus. Every day—often twice a day—a new person showed up.

"Oh, she's hard of hearing? I didn't know that." And then the new aide would try to wrestle the hearing aid in and Lora would get abusive.

We found a doctor for her. David Liederman's cousin is married to a hospital administrator, who recommended a woman who specializes in elder care. The Liedermans, at this point, were back at our house in Umbria, drinking our wine, cooking in our wood-burning oven, and eating all the vegetables out of our garden. Finding us a doctor was the least they could do.

The doctor examined Lora—both physically and mentally. She asked Lora questions similar to those the nurse had asked to ascertain her mental capabilities. Then she sent us to a neurologist who delved further into the question of Alzheimer's disease. After some tests, he wasn't yet ready to say that this was the cause of her dementia. Apparently a definite diagnosis of Alzheimer's is impossible without performing an autopsy. What doctors do is try to eliminate all the other possible causes of the dementia and, if there's no other reason, they call it Alzheimer's. With Lora's situation—the recent death of her husband, the bruises to her brain caused by her falling, the wrenching move to New York, which caused so much disorientation—the doctors weren't ready to make such a diagnosis. In time, they said, they'd be able to do that.

Her doctor took Lora off the antianxiety drug. She said that with some patients, this drug can make the situation worse rather than better, and clearly Lora was one of those patients. Then she prescribed an antipsychotic instead. Just hearing the word "psychotic" was difficult for Jill. She wasn't ready to give up yet. She wasn't yet ready to say, "This isn't my mother," as I had done with my mine.

Jill took Lora to the museum—fiercely holding onto the vision of mother and daughter enjoying New York together—but Lora couldn't, or wouldn't, look at anything. If they went down to the lobby to listen to a piano concert or a lecture on the flowers of Riverside Park, Lora was completely unresponsive, almost comatose. Every day, Jill looked into her mother's eyes for forgiveness, and each time Lora looked away.

Here it was—Jill's ancient drama with her mother, "Look at me, Mommy. Please look at me." It's exactly what she was working on in her therapy. Her shrink told her that having her mother three blocks away was like living in a petri dish. All her issues were right in her face. She thought it was a great opportunity for Jill. The shrink, thank God, lives only a block and a half away from us.

We tried bringing people in to visit Lora because she sometimes tried to rise to the occasion. But when Jill brought over a favorite cousin of Lora's, a woman who plays in the orchestra of the New York City Ballet, Lora turned to the wall and refused to even look at her. She completely froze her out. The cousin was shocked at Lora's condition. The last time she'd been with her—not six months earlier—Lora had talked her ear off about music, about philosophy, about the problems of the world.

One night we brought Lora to our apartment for dinner. Joe and Teresa and their kids were there and Joe, who's irresistible just as a condition of life, totally captivated Lora. He courted her. He shone his attention on her and she blossomed under it. She spoke more that night than she had in weeks. Her words weren't sentences, but she got a laugh on every line, which clearly pleased her.

"He's from a big family," said Teresa. "He's crazy for old people."

And so started a love affair. Joe came to visit Lora regularly in the senior center, and whenever he was there she glowed like a young girl. Jill tried to thank him, but he wouldn't hear of it.

"Hey, honey, I'm not doing this for you—really. It's for me. So please don't thank me. I'm having a ball!

Jill got to talking with a man in the lobby of the senior center who was there visiting his mother. He told her that he had had similar problems with different aides shuttling in and out, and so he hired his own.

"They let you do that?"

"They have to. It's the law—as long as the person you hire is a legal resident and has a license from the state."

"So I can bring my own people in?"

He nodded.

"Where do I find them?"

"The internet, Craigslist. It's not that hard. The aides know they can make more money if they hire out directly because the agencies—like the one in this place—take almost half. If we pay seventeen dollars an hour, the aide gets about ten bucks out of that. Or less. So if you hire someone privately and pay her, say, twelve an hour, then everybody wins. Except the agency, of course."

"Wow."

"And the other reason you want to hire your own people is that the agency in this place doesn't accept Medicaid."

"What do you mean?"

"You can't use Medicaid to pay for your mother's care with these people. They just don't accept it. I guess it's too much bureaucracy for them; they'd rather not have to deal with the government if they don't have to. But if you're will-ing to do the legwork, you can hire your own aides and have Medicaid pay them."

Jill said "Wow" a few more times and then ran home to tell me her new plan. The guy had given Jill the name of an attor-ney who specializes in Medicaid and we were in his office two days later.

The most important thing, the lawyer explained, is that we divest Lora of whatever money she has left. If she has money, she doesn't qualify for Medicaid. This would be easy to do because we already had Jill's name on Lora's bank ac-counts, so all Jill had to do was write a check to herself and Lora would be without funds. Then we'd use those funds to pay for her rent, the furniture rental, supplemental medical insurance—all the things that Medicaid won't cover.

Lora had been right when she accused us of trying to take her money. That's exactly what we did. Never mind that we were using it to take care of her; in fact, her worst paranoid fantasy had come true.

In the meantime, we put ads in all the appropriate places—elder care wanted, specialist in dementia preferred —and waited for the phone to ring.

## TWENTY-ONE

# The Kids

ALISON FLEW TO NEW YORK to start looking for a place to live. Her plan was to rent her house in Los Angeles and use the money to pay for her apartment in New York. Then she would set about establishing her business as a private chef on the East Coast.

On her first night in town we all went down to the Lower East Side to see Max play a gig with one of his bands. Typically, the band didn't start until nearly midnight, so once the set was over, Jill and I crawled home to bed. Alison stayed on. God knows when she got home, but the next morning—around noon, actually—she got up and wandered into the kitchen. I put on some coffee and the three of us sat around the counter.

"Max is awesome," she said, with the authority of someone who's a generation younger and hipper than we are. "The band is great and all, but he lifts up the whole room. He really blew me away."

"Did you all go out after?"

"Yeah, Pop. I became an official groupie. Which means I'll have to have sex with all the guys in the band—except Max, of course. It'll be a full-time job."

"You can do it," said Jill. "We have faith in you."

Alison smiled proudly for her mother.

"And . . . I think we're going to find an apartment together. I mean Max and I. Not the band."

"You're kidding," I said. This didn't sound like a good idea to me, at all. "You guys are getting along so well; why ruin it?"

"No, it'll be good. If I can find the right place, I think it'll work for both of us. I'll just feel better about moving here and maybe I can kick his butt a little—in the right direction."

"I think it's great," said Jill.

"Yeah, well, I have to find the place. But I'm meeting an agent this afternoon who has some apartments up in Harlem that might have more room for less money. We'll see."

Alison has always been very sharp with money. When she was in college, she got a part-time job checking coats in a restaurant and told me to stop sending her money. She's always been an independent person. Max, on the other hand, is a musician, so money is more like a vague concept to him.

"What about Dexter?" I asked. Dexter is Alison's dog and we're very fond of him, although he is a singular-looking pooch, very low to the ground. Alison describes him as a German Labradorgie, and that should give you a fair idea of what he looks like.

"I'm giving him to Shannon."

"Wow. Is that hard for you?"

"Yeah, sure. But Dexter's not really a New York kind of guy. He's a surfer dude. I'm going to be busy getting my act together in New York and Shannon loves him. A lot."

"But you've always had a dog around. Are you sure you're going to want to live without one?"

She shrugged. "I'll have Max."

She seemed to have it all thought out.

"So, did he have a date last night?" asked Jill nonchalantly.

"Mom, come on. He's a drummer in a rock band; he doesn't have dates. He's got like lines around the block. All these little girls following him in packs. It's frightening."

Jill nodded. She had to think about that one.

"It's okay, Mom, it's a phase. You will have grandchildren, eventually; don't worry."

Jill smiled. Alison took a moment and then changed gears.

"So, Max said it was weird the last time he saw grandma. He said she can't really talk anymore."

We'd had Lora to dinner, and Max had come over to welcome his grandmother to New York. After all, it had been his idea and he was proud of that. When she saw him, she lit up and he went over to hug her. Then he asked her how she was doing and she couldn't get any words out. Jill tried to cover for her mom, leaping in to answer the question, but Max hadn't been able to hide the shock on his face.

"Well, she was still recovering from those bumps on her head and . . . the move to New York," said Jill. "We've really put her through a tough time."

"Yeah, well, that's what Max said. I'm just the messenger here."

"I was there this morning, but morning's not a good time for her. The aides keep trying to wake her up for breakfast and she's not ready, so she gets hostile."

"Yeah, wow. Who ever thought that grandma was such a bruiser?"

"Come with me later this afternoon, okay? We'll pay a little visit."

"Sure."

Our search for aides was not going well. And neither was Lora's life at the senior center. She had a reputation as a troublemaker, and every time we came to see her, people in the elevator stared at us and raised their eyebrows at each other.

"They're related to the she-devil on the fourth floor," they whispered behind our backs. "You can see it in their eyes."

Lora was refusing to eat the food from the dining room—again, this proved she was completely sane. I brought in care packages from Zabar's and the Chinese restaurant when I could, but her weight loss was alarming. She also refused to take her meds from any of the aides; she was sure they were trying to poison her. Jill was the only person who could get her to take her pills, she was the only person who could get her to eat, and she was the only person who could dress her and get her hearing aid in. Jill was the only person who could keep her alive. How much of this was Lora's manipulation of her daughter? How much of it was Jill's obsession with being the only one who could save her mother? How much of it was the manifestation of her therapist's prophecy that Lora didn't want to die without Jill? Or was it all merely the behavior of a woman in the throes of dementia, without a plan, without an agenda, without any kind of conscious thought?

We desperately needed to find someone to take care of Lora—someone who wasn't Jill. The aides shuttling in and out at the senior center were a mixed bag; they weren't bad people, but most of them had no idea how to handle someone in Lora's condition. We had to find our own people—specialists in the care of dementia patients—and train them to handle Lora's particular needs and quirks. We tried all the Internet sources and interviewed dozens of women, but they were almost all without papers. They told us on the phone they were legal, but when they arrived they couldn't produce the official documents. It seemed the ones with papers and a license were all signed up with the agencies, which we were trying to avoid because they took the lion's share of the money; we wanted the money to go to the person who was helping Lora. We could go the straight Medicaid route, but that meant we would have to take whomever Medicaid sent us, and Jill wasn't ready to give up that kind of control. The lawyer explained that there was something Medicaid called "consumer directed" care. This meant that the consumer—Jill in this case—could hire aides of her own choice and have them paid through Medicaid as long as they qualified under the guidelines. It's a complicated procedure, and you have to find the aides first before you can even apply.

Jill and Alison went to see Lora that evening. I stayed home and cooked dinner. In truth, whenever I could avoid going over there, I did. I'm not proud of this. I would like to have been a more supportive husband and son-in-law but I found the place crushingly depressing and the smell coming up from the kitchen more than I could bear. I went when I had to, and that was that.

When Alison and Jill came back to the apartment, their faces were grim. I put dinner on the table—chicken *scarpariello,* a favorite of Alison's since she was a kid: small pieces of chicken, on the bone, sautéed in oil, then finished in a sauce of garlic, white wine, and rosemary. But neither of them had much appetite.

"So," I ventured, "how's Grandma?"

Alison looked at Jill; she didn't quite know what to say.

"Well, hmm. I don't know. Not too good, I guess. I mean I wouldn't be happy in that place either."

She pushed her food around the plate.

"Do you think she would have been better off if we had left her in Santa Barbara?" asked Jill.

"No. I mean, I don't know. I don't think what you did—or do—has that much to do with it. I think she's just losing it and that's sad. But you didn't do it."

Alison's doing my job again, I thought. She's trying to bring Jill into reality about this whole mess. When I tried to tell Jill the same thing, she would nod but it didn't actually go in. She didn't trust me on this. She was sure that I was just thinking of myself, trying to protect my own life. And she wasn't wrong. But having Alison back me up at least made her think twice about it. The therapist helped a lot, too. When Jill came back from a session, she seemed to be aware of her denial. She actually called herself on it. Her shrink was driving home the same message—that her mom is living out her own destiny and Jill can't save her from it. But the moment she got back with Lora, she couldn't help reacting to any sign she thought she was getting. If Lora smiled at her, then Jill had a good day. "Mom smiled today, she's coming back, she knows what's going on." If Lora was distant or vague, Jill's day was ruined. "Mom's angry at me, she thinks I should be with her more, she feels I'm abandoning her."

I just backed off after a while. I figured that Jill had a therapist and she had to work it through in her own way, in her own time. But it was weird not being on the same wavelength. Over the years I had gotten used to being the one who took care of things for her, who gave her what she needed when she needed it—especially my opinion. But now if I said what I thought, I was the enemy. So either I could join her in the lie or just keep my mouth shut. Not easy for me.

Alison found a great apartment in Harlem that would be perfect for her and Max. So she stepped up her schedule and decided to make her move to New York as soon as possible— whether or not she had rented her place in Los Angeles.

Before she went back to pack up, we threw a couple of dinner parties at our apartment for friends who might be interested in hiring a private chef—either for their own family meals or for dinner parties, cocktail parties, and the like. That's what Alison does best—meals for families or small groups, where she can personalize the food.

The dinners were a smash success. The first night, we had Joe and Teresa and three other couples, and Alison put on a Mexican extravaganza. We started out with first-class margaritas served along with homemade chips, salsa, and guacamole. Then we took our seats at the table and tucked into skirt steak fajitas, cheese enchiladas with a fantastic mole sauce, and grilled marinated chicken tossed in a salad of greens, grilled corn, salsa, and Cojita cheese. We finished up with Mexican coffee and Alison's justly famous key lime pie. Our friends didn't know what had hit them—other than the margaritas, of course. This was much better Mexican food than any of us were used to getting in New York restaurants. The following night, we had four different couples and an all-Indian dinner: potato and spring pea samosas with a mango chutney, homemade naan, chicken Makhani, which is a butter chicken, delicate and easy on the palate, then a lamb vindaloo, which was the opposite—spicy, fiery, and totally satisfying. Our friends all took Alison's card and told her they couldn't wait until she hit town. Frankly, neither could I.

# TWENTY-TWO

# Marcia

SOMETIMES, when a problem seems hopelessly complicated and virtually unsolvable—like Saturday's crossword
puzzle in the *New York Times* with empty spaces all over the
grid—one element falls into place and the whole impen-
etrable mess is suddenly clear as glass and laughingly simple.
That's what happened when Marcia walked through the door.

She came to us through a consultant whom Jill had hired,
a woman specializing in the myriad complications of Medicaid. Although this woman doesn't usually function as an
agency—she doesn't place care workers—she called Jill
about Marcia, who had recently worked for a former client.
When Marcia showed up at our apartment, she showed us
her papers and referrals, which were impeccable, and then
she sat down and took over the interview.

"Tell me about your mom," she said in her soft Jamaican
accent, and Jill poured out the whole story to her—Ralph's
death, the bumps on the head, the hospitalization, the move to
New York, the belligerence, the precipitous fall into dementia.

"So, only a month or so ago, she was taking care of herself? Bathing herself and putting herself to bed?"

"Yes," said Jill. "She was completely independent. She was talking about going back to work."

Marcia smiled.

"Can you imagine what it must be like for her to be suddenly handled by strangers? I'm sure they're trying to wash her, yes? In her most private places? Of course she's hitting."

Jill nodded. "She's incontinent now and she's always wet. But she won't let them get near her."

"Those girls, the aides from the agency, it's not their fault. They're underpaid and overworked and because the agency likes to run them in and out, they have no real chance to get to know the person they're supposed to care for. So they let her lie there in the wet, hopin' that the next person will change her. I know, I was one of them when I first came here. I saw it all. This business is all about trust; you don't have the trust of your person, you can't do nothin'. This whole profession is about earnin' their trust."

Marcia (three syllables, soft "c", accent on the first syllable) is a tall drink of water. One gets the impression that when she was a bit younger, she resembled those extraordinarily beautiful Jamaican athletes we see in the Olympics. The only thing that keeps her from being a classic beauty is the puckish, knowing expression on her face, which instantly tells you everything you need to know about her—that she can find humor in any situation that comes her way and that you don't want to be on the other side of an argument with her. Her eyes have a kind of weary strength that says, *I've been here, I've seen it, and I know what's right.* She grew up in Jamaica, and when she was in her teens her grandfather was diagnosed with a bad cancer. She daily watched her mother nurse him all the way to the end. She remembers being aware of the smell of the tumor on his shoulder as the cancer advanced, the smell of impending death.

"That's when I knew I wanted to do this. I wanted to take care of the old people. They know so much; you can learn everything from them."

She came to the states for her training. First she got her Certified Nursing Assistant certificate, which licensed her to work in nursing homes. She quickly learned that she couldn't do what she wanted in that system.

"The first thing they do is drug them up. The old people come in and they're confused and terrified. They've just had an operation or, like your mom, a fall—and if they make any trouble at all, there's a doctor who's on staff there that gives the drugs. But these drugs are more for the aides than they are for the patients. They just want them quiet and docile so they can do their work and get out. All they thinkin' about is gettin' to the weekend. Is your mom on drugs?"

"Well, she was taking an antianxiety medication that her doctor in Santa Barbara gave her, but we took her off it because it was having the opposite effect. But her doctor here— not the doctor at the senior center, but her own doctor—just put her on an antipsychotic."

"And how is that?"

"It's too soon to tell. She just started it."

Marcia nodded and said nothing, but her concern about the drugs was all over her face.

"So, after I realized that I didn't want to work in that system, I went back to school and got my Home Health Aide certification. Then I was licensed to go into people's homes and take care of them in a more personal way."

"My mom's hard of hearing and that makes everything more difficult. I think it's hard to get her trust if she can't hear you."

"What's her name?

"Lora."

"That's a nice name."

"Would you like to meet her?"

"If you promise me she's not goin' to beat me up."

She smiled at Jill with a glint in her eye, and the whole room got warmer and brighter. I noticed that Jill's shoulders dropped about six inches.

The three of us went over to the senior center and had a meeting with the head nurse at the care agency. Jill had already told her we were thinking of bringing in our own aides, and we had to present Marcia's certification before she would be allowed to go up to the room to meet Lora. Jill and I waited outside while the two of them spoke, and when Marcia came out she told us that the nurse had warned her.

"She told me that your mom is trouble, that the whole place has had trouble with her."

We went upstairs and found Lora still in bed. She rarely got up early. An aide from the agency was there, sitting in a chair across the room. She told us that Lora had refused to get up to go to breakfast. Marcia told her that she could take a break and get some coffee. The aide looked at Jill, who nodded, and then the aide left. Then Marcia pulled a chair up close to the bed—but not too close.

"Where's her hearing aid?" she asked Jill.

Jill found it in the bedside table and handed it to her. Marcia leaned forward with her elbows on her knees and looked Lora in the eye. For a long time they stared at each other. Marcia smiled at her and nodded for a while. Then she held up the hearing aid, pointed to it and then pointed to her ear. No words. Lora stared at her like a puppy that had been abused, never taking her eyes off Marcia for a second. Then Marcia repeated the gesture—as if she were playing charades. And finally Lora responded. She put a fierce frown on her face and shook her head vehemently. No fucking way you're going to put that thing in my ear.

Marcia threw her head back and howled with laughter. She laughed until tears came to her eyes.

"*No?* You don't want this thing?"

And Lora shook her head again, but there was the tiniest hint of interest in her eyes. Marcia got up and took the hearing aid over to the trash can, gesturing to indicate that she could put it in there.

"Should I throw it away?"

And Lora nodded vigorously; she now had a smile on her face.

"Okay." And Marcia—gently—dropped the hearing aid into the trash.

At this point, all four of us were laughing.

"Why don't you guys go out for a while. Give us some time and then maybe bring back something nice for her breakfast. Bring her everything she likes."

We came back about an hour later with some breakfast. Lora was washed and dressed, she had her makeup on, and was looking great. And she had her hearing aid in.

"She don't have the Alzheimer's," said Marcia when we came through the door. "She's got a fine brain."

"Did she give you any trouble?"

"Oh, sure. She's got very particular ways to do things, so

I have to learn. She wants to be the boss. She don't want to be told nothin'."

We hung around for a while, watching Marcia seduce Lora into eating her breakfast. Whenever Lora balked, Marcia made her laugh; the laughter made Lora forget what she was resisting—and down went the breakfast. It was dazzling.

"You guys go home. I'll do the rest of the day. I'm hired, right?"

We both nodded.

"I can't do the twenty-four hours, you know, 'cause I have two kids. And a husband—sometimes. So you'll need another girl for the night and then someone for the weekends. You know that, right?"

We nodded again.

"But don't worry. I'll train everybody. We'll get it runnin' like a cruise ship. Lolo is the queen and we all goin' to make her happy."

"Lolo?"

"That's what I call her. Lolo. We goin' to the park after breakfast, so you guys can go on home."

"Her wheelchair is in the closet, folded up," said Jill.

"No. I think we're goin' to walk a little. She's got to get the blood movin'."

In less than a week we had the other two aides signed up. We were free of the agency. Jill got busy to get them all cleared for Medicaid. They needed to have their papers checked to make sure they were legal residents and certified, and they all had to have a physical checkup. In the meantime, Jill watched Marcia take the full weight of Lora's care onto her shoulders. Marcia took it gracefully. It wasn't a burden for her, she was born for it. Jill, I think, was confused at first. After the angst of the recent months, it was difficult for her to let go of the responsibility. But slowly she started to trust Marcia—and she relaxed her grip.

Over the next couple of months, Marcia became more important to Lora than Jill was. Even though Jill was— is—Lora's only daughter, even though she had cradled Lora through her most difficult time, when she was abandoned and bereft, and even though a big part of Jill's very identity has been tied up with her responsibility for her mother, Marcia was able to give Lora something that Jill couldn't give. She was able to love Lora—Lolo to her—as Lora was now. She had no expectation of seeing the former Lora, the intellectual, the elegant hostess, the mother, the grandmother; she had never known that Lora. She had none of Jill's disappointment and frustration, none of Jill's sadness for the Lora who used to be. She knew only Lolo. And she loved her.

"Could I take her off the drugs?" Marcia asked one day. "I was in the park and Lolo was sleeping in her chair and another girl came up to me and told me that my lady was sleepin' too much. She's right. It can't be good for her. If she sleeps so much, she just gonna curl up and die. I've seen it before."

"Let me talk to her doctor," said Jill.

The doctor was fine about it. She said we shouldn't do it all at once, but very slowly—lessening the dose over a period of weeks. Marcia nodded and agreed.

The fear—our fear—was that Lora would go back to her belligerent behavior and become a social problem at the senior center. Before Marcia came on board, Lora had been known to leave her apartment in the middle of the night and bang on the doors of other residents. The agency's aides had been too intimidated to stop her. We were warned a number of times that if she didn't stop annoying the other residents she would be asked to leave the building. Marcia saw the problem another way.

"It's not the drugs that's keeping her from that bad behavior. It's that she's being treated with respect. She still doin' it sometimes. She yells at me and tries to hit me if I try to make her do something she don't want to do. But then I just make her laugh and it all goes away. It's not the drugs that's doin' it. The drugs are just makin' her brain slow."

We told her to try it—to start weaning Lora off of the antipsychotic meds. We had a unique situation—a caretaker who wanted her difficult patient off the drugs rather than on drugs—and we thought we should take advantage of it.

The process took about three weeks, and there were difficult times along the way. Kethleen, Lora's nighttime aide, sometimes had problems in the middle of the night when Lora would wake up disoriented. Lora would get out of bed and try to escape from the room, and there was nothing Kethleen could say to calm her. They ended up having wrestling matches. On Marcia's recommendation, Kethleen tried letting Lora win the argument.

"She want to go out into the hall, okay. Get her dressed. Remind her she can't go outside in her night clothes. Get her dressed and take her where she wants to go. Let her know she's the boss."

Kethleen walked the halls with her, taking her down in the elevator to the lobby in the middle of the night and walking her back and forth until she calmed herself. Finally she would be able to get back to sleep.

"The next thing would be to get her out of this place," said Marcia. "This building is poison to her. Everybody looks at her like she have the evil eye and that's not good for her health, you know?"

## TWENTY-THREE

# Closer to Home

ON MY WAY HOME ONE AFTERNOON—I had been downtown auditioning for the voice-over in a dog food commercial —I was letting myself into my apartment when a young couple came out of the door across the hall. They were followed by the real estate guy who had sold us our apartment a few years before. He waved to me and I waved back and after he said good-bye to the couple I asked him what was going on.

"We're having an open house today for 3B. I've been showing it all day."

"What is it? A one-bedroom?"

"Yeah. About half the size of your place."

"What are they asking for it?

I'm a real estate junkie and I always have an eye out for the ups and downs of the New York real estate market. Whereas home prices had been dropping all over the country, New York apartments had so far been holding their value.

"No, it's a rental. It's one of the sponsor apartments."

Our building is a co-op. It's a seven-story prewar structure on a pleasant, middle-class block on the Upper West Side. Most of the apartment owners have lived here a long time and were around when the building was converted from rental to co-op. But there were a few apartments—five or six in the whole building—that, for one reason or another, weren't bought by their residents. These were picked up by a real estate speculator and rented out on yearly leases. They're called sponsor apartments.

"What's the rent?"

He showed me the flyer. The apartment was renting for exactly half the price that Lora was paying per month for her studio apartment at the senior center. Of course, the price at the center included other things—three meals a day; social amenities like the clubs, the lectures, and the trips to the museums; the lobby security: and access to the care agency in the building—none of which Lora was taking advantage of. I took the flyer, tucked it into my pocket, and said nothing about it to Jill when I saw her later that afternoon. I had to think about it. On the one hand, it would solve a lot of our problems, or it could be my worst nightmare come true.

Our apartment is the smallest space Jill and I have lived in since we were starving actors breaking into the New York theater in the early 1970s. It's the cornerstone of our attempt to "downsize" our life as we take our pensions and enter our retirement years—or semiretirement years, because an actor never really retires. For an actor of advancing age, there's always the role of a grandfather in a play or the role of a burned-out wino in a movie, a small role that doesn't have a lot of lines to memorize. But since there's no money to be made in the theater and even less playing small roles in films, we act for the love of it while, financially speaking, we're *in pensione,* as the Italians say. Our apartment is a symbol of this chapter in our lives, a metaphor—small, not lavish, a nice place to touch down when we're in New York, a pied-à-terre for when we're not in Italy at our real retirement house. We like it this way. It's cozy and romantic; it reminds us of when we were first together and didn't need fancy things around us to have fun. After the years in Hollywood, this feels good to us.

But if we move Lora and her twenty-four-hour aides in across the hall, our apartment will become the clubhouse. It's inevitable. Jill is a magnet. Everyone wants to be with her. So, she'll be running her mother's entire operation from our little living room and my quiet Jewish-scholar world—my peace, my solitude—will be demolished. I like to write every day. I like to make my coffee first thing in the morning, read the *New York Times,* and then start work at my makeshift desk at the kitchen counter while Jill does her morning ritual, which consists of a walk in the park, then a little Pilates, then stretching, then yoga, and finally her meditation. It's developed into at least a one-hour regime before her breakfast. This gives me a beautiful space to get past whatever blocks I woke up with and get a page or two into what I'm working on. Beautiful, serene space.

Then there's my life's other passion, which is basically lying on my back on the couch, reading the latest *New Yorker*. It corresponds to our siesta time in Italy, where we first learned how to nap. After a big lunch and a bottle of wine, we would go to our respective spots. Jill's is our bedroom where she turns on her ambient sound machine, hooks up her alpha-wave machine buds to her earlobes, and takes her daily *pisolino,* which is Italian for nap; I lie down on the couch—whether we're in Italy or New York, it's always the couch—and start a magazine or a crossword puzzle but quickly dive into a prolonged snore. It's heaven. It's the highlight of my day. They say that naps are one of the great keys to longevity; I'll let you know when I get there.

All this would be taken from me if we moved Lora across the hall. First of all, Jill wouldn't be Jill any more. She'd have this big umbilical cord coming out of her belly button that stretches across the hall into 3B, and I'd be tripping over it all the time. Her obsession would be completely and utterly in my face. She'd be the commander at "action central," with a big map with colored pins on it and time sheets and three phones ringing all the time, and aides running in, reporting to the commander, and asking us to order more diapers. I can't do it. I can't have it.

My secret lasted until dinnertime. I can't keep anything from Jill. I used to be pretty good at it, but not any more. At our age we don't have time for secrets.

"You know that apartment across the hall? 3B?"

"No. Who lives there?"

"That's just it, nobody lives there. They were having an open house earlier today."

"We have an apartment."

"It's a rental, honey. They're renting it for half what we're paying for your mother at the senior center. It's available, it's a good size for her and the aides, it's light, and it has a decent kitchen."

She bit the inside of her lip for a minute and stared at me. Then she shook her head. "I can't do it. It's too close. I think I'd go crazy."

It's extraordinary, I thought, how little I know her. I still get her wrong about 80 percent of the time.

"I thought you wanted to get her out of that place."

"I do. Definitely. But not across the hall. I can't do it."

This was her brain talking, the intelligent, rational part of her psyche. It didn't take long for the other part, the one that lives lower down around the internal organs, to take over the decision-making process. Her resolve to be rational lasted about as long as my secret. After dinner we called the real estate guy and he came over with the key and showed us the apartment.

The living room–kitchen area was about the same size as Lora's entire apartment at the senior center, and there was a decent-size bedroom down the hall. We could set her up in the living room with her bed, the television, the sofa, and the same art, furniture, and photos that she has now, in roughly the same position—and then use the bedroom as a place for the aides to rest as well as for storage for the walker, the wheelchair, and all of Lora's clothes, etcetera. Other than the fact that the bathroom would be a little farther away from her bed, it was perfect. It had a view of the street with trees at her window height and it had light. Perfect.

The real estate guy left us the key so that we could show the apartment to Marcia that night when she ended her shift. She came by and gave it a thumbs-up. She agreed that we should make the living room Lora's area, so that Lora would have to go through as little change as possible. Except for one or two more windows and more light, we could make the layout exactly the same as where she is now.

"Don't you think she'll miss having other people around? Other older people to socialize with?" asked Jill.

"No," said Marcia. "She doesn't want to have anything to do with the people over there."

"But what about guys?" I said. "She might find some geezer who wants to put the move on her. She likes guys."

"The only guy for her is your friend, Joe. She only got eyes for him. And he could come over here just as easy as over there. Easier, right?"

"Joe's married," I pointed out.

"She don't care."

Marcia had a merry smile on her face and she shook her head as if to say, *Love conquers all.* Then she turned to me.

"What about you, Mikey?" She once heard Jill call me by that name and picked it up immediately. "You got a bad look on your face. This is too close for comfort for you."

"No, I'm fine."

"I don't think so. I can see right into your heart, Mikey. You didn't like to come over there, did you? To visit? So now instead we're coming to you. To where you live. I don't think you're so happy about that."

I didn't say anything.

Jill looked over at me to see how this landed. I realized that when she said earlier that she didn't want her mother so close, she was worried about me. She didn't want to lose me on this—my backing, that is. If she had to tap dance between me and her mother, she would lose her mind. And I was in a similar kind of limbo—sure, I would back her if I could figure out what the hell she wanted, but she was all over the place. Did she really want her mother so close, or was she terrified of it? Both, it seemed. This was old, murky, mother-swamp territory for her and even with the help of her therapist, she was struggling for her footing. And when Jill's not solid, I'm lost; I'm on a little, rickety raft in the middle of the ocean, trying to see over the swells.

"Don't worry, Mikey," said Marcia. "I'll protect you. I'll make sure you keep your space."

I nodded. Jill nodded. Marcia, at least, seemed to know what she wanted.


I was on the phone with Alison the next day. She would be making her move to New York in a few days, and she was very excited. She hadn't rented her house in Los Angeles yet, but she was going to leave it to the real estate agent and come ahead anyway. Max had given his roommate notice and would be moving in on the same day as Alison. I told her about the apartment across the hall and the new situation with Lora.

"Wow. That's cutting it kind of close, isn't it?"

I told her it was the only way that Jill would be able to keep an eye on things, and at this point, she needed to do that.

"What are you going to do about her food?"

"Well, anything will be an improvement. Even if we just had Chinese carry-out, she'd eat better than she's eating now."

"Well, you know, there's a rumor that a really good personal chef is going to be moving into your neighborhood in a couple of days. I hear she has fantastic references. I also hear she's in dire need of a job."

Duh.

"You know, Dad, usually I don't do all that fancy ethnic food I cooked for your friends. Most of my clients in Hollywood are health freaks. I don't think I have any women clients out here who weigh more than a hundred pounds. Mostly I cook very, very fresh, very, very healthy, very, very slimming food—and then I make it taste great so that everybody's happy. I can talk to Grandma's doctor and find out exactly what's best for her and then turn that into comfort food. That's my specialty."

"Sold. You got the job."

"Great. I need a job. I'm a little terrified about this whole thing. I talked to Max, by the way, and he's all set."

"Yeah, I spoke with him, too."

"See you in a couple of days, Pop."

I hung up and thought about how our family was gathering close together—almost on top of each other. It was all getting very Italian.

# TWENTY-FOUR

# La Famiglia

THE ITALIAN CONSTITUTION STATES that the basic unit is the family—not the individual. So the difference between the American and Italian attitudes toward family and the care of aging parents is not just cultural or traditional—it's the law. There are nursing homes in Italy, and there are assisted-care centers and senior housing facilities; but very few families take advantage of them. It's considered shameful in Italy for families not to have their aging parents at home. More often it's the parents' home that everyone ends up living in. Many of the children—people in their forties or fifties—have never left. When they get married, they just move their spouse and subsequent offspring into the family home. The parents usually own their house, which has been passed down through the generations; their pension is generous, especially if they worked for the government; if they're in business or farming, the enterprise is usually family-operated and run out of the home, free of rent or mortgage. So, for economic as well as cultural and legal reasons, Italian families stick together; they take care of their own. We've seen virtually no homeless people in our area of Umbria, because the mentally ill are usually taken in and cared for by the family, as opposed to being put into an institutional situation or tossed out onto the street to fend for themselves.

In recent years, because of growing urbanization, children have sought help to care for their parents. *Badanti,* or caregivers—often immigrants from eastern Europe—are playing a bigger and bigger role. They work backbreaking hours—usually twenty-four hours a day, six days a week—for very little pay, and they are becoming invaluable to the system. There was such an uproar over recent strict immigration laws that special provisions were added to the legislation so as not to jeopardize the supply of *badanti*. The system is not dissimilar to the one in New York, where we have a large and relatively inexpensive army of caregivers from Jamaica, Haiti, and the other Caribbean islands attending to both the young children and the aged parents of busy two-career families. The difference is that in Italy the care of the old is done primarily in the home rather than in an institutional setting, whereas the reverse is true in the states. For whatever reasons, we Americans want our elderly to be in places where we can't see them, but the Italians, whether by choice or necessity, live with their old folks and mingle with them on a daily basis. In Italy there are always three, sometimes four generations hanging around each other. So they live in a continuum of births and deaths and all the steps in between. Maybe this is why the Italians are so good at enjoying life; they don't try to avoid the fact that it's finite.

All this was running through my mind as I watched my family Italianize before my eyes. We moved Lora in across the hall and her aides, led by Marcia, covered her around the clock in shifts. Alison and Max moved into their apartment just uptown from us. Max, who was gigging in New York at least two nights a week, would often come home at four in the morning and discover a treat left by his big sister, the chef. One night there was an eggplant parmigiano hero sandwich waiting for him on the kitchen counter, on rosemary bread fresh-baked by Alison. Jill quipped, "He'll never get married."

Often as not on a Sunday, Alison attended Max's church gig in Harlem. No matter how busy Max was with his other bands, and no matter how late he got to bed on Saturday night, he would always manage to wake up in time to play with the gospel trombone choir at the United House of Prayer on Sunday. He also liked to hang out socially with the other young men in the group, and Alison sometimes joined in. The 'boners, as she likes to call them, are apparently a fun group.

"Why don't you guys meet me there this Sunday?" Alison asked us. "Then we'll all get some lunch afterward."

We hadn't been to the church for three or four years—not since Max first started playing there. I've never been much interested in organized religion of any kind; I'm not an organized kind of guy. And Jill, too, tends to take her spirituality in a personal rather than a congregational way. But whether you end up embracing Jesus or not, the service at the United House of Prayer is an uplifting and rousing way to spend a Sunday morning, so we agreed to meet Alison.

Even though we dressed up a bit—I had on a freshly ironed shirt and nice pants rather than my usual jeans and golf shirt—we were by far the least best-dressed people in church. The men all wore dark suits, starched white shirts, and ties; the ladies wore lovely dresses with stockings and high heels—all accessorized to the max. We weren't the only white people in attendance that day—there were three or four others—but we were instantly recognized as Max's family and warmly greeted at the door. The women, who seem to be in charge of running the show, are gracious and welcoming hosts. And they all wear great hats.

The musicians start the proceedings—seven or eight trombones, a tuba, a snare drum, and cymbals—and they play pretty much through the entire service, which goes on for three hours or so. Their sound is a precursor to New Orleans funeral music, but even older and more closely connected to its African roots. It is as undeniable as any music you've ever experienced. It doesn't enter your body through your ears; rather it directly engages your internal organs. Your body moves whether you ask it to or not, it's impossible to sit still, and you can't not clap and march and sway. And when the preacher calls out for you to praise the Lord, you praise Him. You can't not praise Him. The rhythm is eternal; it's elemental. After a while, some of the parishioners enter ecstatic states. Some fall to the floor and writhe; some speak in tongues. The music has taken them to another level of consciousness. The wonderful women with the hats gather around whoever goes into ecstasy and make sure that people don't hurt themselves in any way while they're out-of-body. It's quite a scene. And, in the middle of the band, driving the sound, is our tall, slender white boy, banging his cymbals together, marching in place while the trombones are swaying back and forth. The cymbals must weigh at least ten pounds apiece, and Max clashes them together with such exuberance that I wonder that his arms don't fall off. He and the other players, the 'boners, went on in this altered state for hours, which is a nice way for kids to get high.

The sermon that Sunday was a passionate diatribe against the evils of television. The preacher made a strong case against being addicted to this infernal machine, which blares out false values, displays unattainable body images, and importunes you to buy products you don't need or want. He made a great case. Afterward, we went up to thank him for the service and he apologized to us—one of the women had whispered to him that we had made our living on television. We told him that no apology was necessary, that we couldn't have agreed more. He told us that Max is a fine young man, and we answered that we were aware of this.

Our little family was expanding. Marcia, because she was employed full-time with us, was able to get her son, Keyshawn, into the public elementary school in our neighborhood. She thought it was a better school than the one out where she lived. Her shift started at eight in the morning, so she and Keyshawn took the subway in together from Brooklyn; she dropped him at school and came to work. At three o'clock, Marcia bundled up Lora, put her in the wheelchair, and walked the three blocks or so to pick up Keyshawn. Then he'd come back with them to the apartment and do his homework at the table in Lora's kitchen. At first Lora seemed jealous of Keyshawn, and she would regularly take a swing at him if he got too close. But he had a good sense of humor about it and eventually Lora adopted a more accepting attitude toward him, sometimes acting grandmotherly but more often acting like another nine-year-old. After his homework, they would have their afternoon snack together and then watch some television. When Jill came over to visit, Lora would point at Keyshawn with an amazed look on her face and say, "Look at that!"

One afternoon, Marcia was taking Lora to a doctor's appointment and Jill had an audition, so they asked me if I would pick up Keyshawn at school and bring him back to the apartment. No problem. On the way home I asked if he was hungry, and of course he was, so I took him into Zabar's, which, for those of you who don't know New York, is perhaps the pre-eminent deli in the world. Keyshawn was dazzled by the display of food, and he eventually picked out a bagel to eat on the way home.

"You're rich, Mikey," he said, adopting Marcia's nickname for me. "You're really rich." Amazing how much respect can be bought with a sesame seed bagel.

Alison was over at our place cooking for Lora a couple of times a week, using our kitchen, which has more space and is better equipped than the one in Lora's apartment. There were some perks involved with this arrangement: my kitchen was subtly reorganized and re-equipped over time —all the changes were improvements—and I was now properly stocked at all times. I never had to worry whether I had fresh garlic or onions, there was always a supply of home-made chicken stock in the fridge, and there was also always a squeeze bottle of something Alison calls "gooey," which is a chef's mixture of scallions, parsley, garlic, olive oil, and pepper, emulsified in the Cuisinart. You can use it as a marinade or a coating for roasted or grilled meats, or add it to sautéed vegetables—whatever. If Alison bakes bread for Lora, she'll do an extra loaf for us. Ditto for some of her most popular dishes—there's often some extra turkey meat loaf with roasted potatoes waiting to be warmed up for lunch or for a quick dinner when we're in a rush. And there's her key lime pie, which is purely and simply the best key lime pie in the world. There's often a wedge or two on the top shelf in the fridge.

The downside is that Jill and I have less privacy. Alison has her own key and comes in two or three times a week to cook or get a shopping list from Lora's aides. Once she walked in when Jill and I were in the bedroom grabbing a nooner, and after an embarrassed moment she recommended we throw the dead bolt when we don't want to be interrupted and she'll just take a walk in the park until we're done.

When she first started cooking at our place, often as not I'd be home, perched at my spot at the kitchen counter with my laptop, writing or wasting time on the Internet. I'd watch as she prepped her dishes and I'd ask her questions about them; I figured I could learn something. But I noticed that I was making her nervous. It was hard for her to cook in front of me. Then a month or so later I noticed that her nervousness had disappeared.

"You're not bothered by having me watch you cook anymore. You've changed. I think you've gotten more confidence."

She thought about that for a second. "I think you're the one who's changed."

As I said, Alison's really smart. She nailed me. What made her nervous at first was that she sensed I wasn't very happy having her in my kitchen—I felt invaded and proprietary. Sure, I was fine at romanticizing the Italians and their way of life, but when it came to myself, I was as American as apple pie. I wanted my family around only when it was convenient for me. But as Alison further perceived, I went through a change. After a month or two of having her around in the kitchen, I got into it and realized that I could enjoy this new intimacy with my daughter. It wasn't by choice, because, believe me, I don't change easily. It was because of forces beyond my control—Jill's needs, Lora's needs, my kids' needs, Marcia's needs—that I was dragged kicking and screaming into an extended family life.

There's a tiny store in Poreta, the little town within walking distance of our house in Italy. Poreta has only one store, which is a little catch-as-catch-can *alimentari* with some fresh garden vegetables, some milk, some cheese, and a few canned goods—the local version of a 7-Eleven. Jill walked over there one day to buy some apples and found the woman who owned the place in the midst of restocking her shelves. Jill gave her the obligatory, "Buongiorno" as she entered the store, and the woman shouted back, "Cows! Tutto cows."

Jill bought the apples and walked home and told me about this strange expression she had heard—"Cows! All cows." We called Martin, who, although German, speaks the local dialect fluently. He laughed.

"No, Michael. Not cows. Chaos. Remember, the Italians pronounce all the vowels. Ch is the hard 'c'; 'a' 'o' 's.' Chaos."

That's what I have tramping through my New York apartment these days—a big herd of chaos.

# TWENTY-FIVE

# Jill

HAVING HER MOM ACROSS THE HALL did not make things easier for Jill. Rather, it intensified her feelings of responsibility. When her mother had been even a few blocks away from us, Jill had been able to leave for short periods of time, letting the aides handle things. But now there was no break; her every moment was fraught with guilt and anxiety. The anxiety was well founded. In the senior center there had always been a registered nurse on duty in case a medical emergency arose. Now we would just have our aides, who were trained and certified but not to that level. Of course we could go to the emergency room at a hospital if we needed to, but there was a responsibility that fell on Jill's shoulders that hadn't been there before. Essentially, what we were doing was setting up our own little nursing home in the apartment across the hall. And Jill was running it.

The guilt was more complicated. Jill couldn't get comfortable with the fact that Lora was right across the hall and not in our apartment all the time. She knew in her head that the separation was necessary but she couldn't stop feeling guilty about it.

"My mother is sitting watching television with a relative stranger while her only daughter is just steps away. I'm here—just across the hall. This is crazy!" She didn't say this, but she was thinking it.

Almost every night she would bring Lora over to our place and prop her up on a bar stool at the kitchen counter while I was cooking dinner. Jill would show her a poem or a letter from an old acquaintance, and Lora would read it over and over. I'd make her some tea and she'd sit there with a lost expression on her face, trying to look good, as if she was on top of things. Then after a while it became clear that she was exhausted and Jill would take her back across the hall where she didn't have to pretend to be anything. It wasn't Lora's need to socialize with us in our apartment, it was Jill's.

When Jill wasn't obsessing about her mom, she worried about the aides—about their welfare, their families, their salaries. She got involved with the aides' children, writing letters of recommendation for their schools and job applications. She worried when Lora was difficult or belligerent and treating the aides badly. She worried about Alison and how she interfaced with the aides. She worried about the responsibilities of dealing with Medicaid. She worried about me, of course. I was the one who was exhorting her to separate from her mom, to let the aides do their job, to focus on herself and her own life. But this was not the message she wanted to hear at that point. She was not ready to walk away.

Jill is counterphobic. This means that when she's confronted by something terrifying, challenging, or potentially painful, she puts her head down and charges right into it. Then she sumo wrestles with it—for months, sometimes years—until she vanquishes it. That's my Jill. So, when her therapist pointed out that having her mother across the hall was a perfect opportunity for her to grapple with her most basic issues, Jill grappled away with her customary enthusiasm. She read all the books and did all the exercises.

The issues—without getting overly psychological about it—could be summarized as, "Notice me, notice me, Mommy" and "I'm the only one who can save you." Neither of these concepts was a realistic expectation to have for a mother who was sinking into dementia. The shrink maintained that the reactions and emotions Jill was feeling were those of the little girl rather than of the mature woman. And being able to clearly see the difference was the key to conquering the problem.

This is great stuff. I'm a believer. I love therapy—I've done a lot of it myself. Jill, I know, will work diligently and eventually conquer these patterns, which go all the way back to her childhood, and she'll able to live fully in the present as her wonderful and glorious self. In the meantime, however, she was driving me out of my fucking mind.

I, too, am counterphobic. Except for the counter part. When I see something scary or painful approaching, I hang a quick left, drive around the block, and park in an inconspicuous place until whatever it is goes away. I go straight forward only for pleasure. If I have to experience pain for any reason, I try to forget about it as quickly as possible. Given our temperaments, it's amazing to think that Jill and I have been able to stay together for all these years. Or maybe the difference explains it. We certainly don't duplicate each other.

In the middle of all this turmoil, the phone rang. This is what happens in an actor's life—the phone rings and life or destiny, or whatever you want to call it, takes you in a whole new direction.

This time it wasn't a job, really. More like a gig. One of the big cruise lines was offering us a free cruise and first-class

round-trip airfare if we did one performance of *Love Letters*—
a wonderful two-character play by A. R. Gurney—on one of
the nights when the ship was at sea. The deal was that the
cruise line would fly us to Istanbul, where we'd spend a day
or two, then we'd cruise around Turkey, the Greek Islands,
Taormina in Sicily, and Naples, and then finish up in Rome,
which is only an hour and a half from our house in Umbria.
We could then spend a couple of weeks at the house and watch
the spring come in. We'd hike up the mountain to a high
meadow where we can walk over a carpet of wildflowers and
see the snowcapped Sibilini in the distance. It would still be
cool enough to have the fireplace going in the dining room
and I'd do a pork roast rubbed with garlic and rosemary—I'd
have it turning on the spit over the wood coals in the fireplace
and our little house would fill up with the smell. We'd see our
pals and hang out at the Palazzaccio, lingering for hours in the
intoxicating mix of food, wine, and friends. Oh, God, I hadn't
even let myself think this way for months. I'd blocked it out.
Either I'm in the pleasure mode or I'm not—if I can't access it,
I shut the system down; the taste buds, the smell buds, the
sex buds, they all take a break. But this phone call woke them
all up.

The problem was that Jill wasn't yet ready to leave her
mother long enough to go out to dinner, even up to the corner for a burger or something—much less fly to Turkey. Jill
actually fielded the call about the cruise, which came from
her agent. After she briefed me on the offer she said, "It's a
shame. If it was different timing, this would be a lot of fun."

So in her mind it was dead. No way, José.

"Did you turn it down?"

"Well, I wanted to talk to you about it first, but I don't
see how we could do it. Maybe next year."

"Why next year? What's going to be different next year?"

"Oh, come on, honey. This operation is still very shaky here. I'm not at all sure about the third aide, the one who covers the weekends—Annette. I don't think that she really gets my mom, and she's always complaining that she can't go to church on Sunday. She's not happy doing weekends."

"Then why did she take the job? The job was weekends."

"Exactly."

"So replace her."

"It's not easy. Everybody tells me that finding someone for the weekends is the hardest thing. They all want to go to church and be with their families. I'd have to find someone who's certified and legal, then I'd have to get her cleared by Medicaid. It would be a big deal. And Marcia thinks that she can whip Annette into shape. She and Kethleen will cover some of the Sundays so that Annette can go to church sometimes. We're working it out, but I can't do it from Turkey."

"Okay." I know I can't push. I can put the menu out there and wait for her to bite. Or not. This time not.

"Okay," I said again. "Call your agent and tell him we can't do it."

But she didn't. She put it off. There was something in her that wanted nothing more in the world than to fly to a very distant place and get on a ship and sail out into the ocean where she would have space and spaciousness. Part of her wanted exactly this, and the universe had just dropped it into her lap. When the universe speaks, Jill listens.

She went to her therapist, who urged her to take the trip.

"You have to live your life," the therapist told her. "Your mother—if she were really your mother, in her right mind—would want you to go."

This was one of the big themes Jill was working on—that she has put her needs and desires aside in order to accommodate her mother, even if her mother wasn't asking her to do it. Here was a chance to turn that around.

She came home from the therapist with her head spinning. Alison was in the kitchen prepping some vegetables, and I was at the counter, having a coffee.

"My shrink says I should do the cruise."

"Double her fee!" I chipped in.

"Of course you should do the cruise," said Alison. "Are you kidding?"

"I don't know how I can, honey. I'd be a mess, worrying about everything."

"I'll be you."

Jill just looked at her.

"I'll do the Jill part. I'll pop over there every day and check on things, I'll be in touch with Marcia constantly, I'll fill out the Medicaid forms and make sure they sign them, that's easy—I've watched you do it. I'll keep the weekend broad in line. Then I'll e-mail you every day and tell you that everything's okay. They have e-mail on the ship, right?"

"Honey . . ."

I started to mist up, which is not saying much—I cry at card tricks—but this was very moving to me. Alison was trying to underplay it, just matter-of-factly saying that she could cover, but it was more than that. This was Alison saying thank you to Jill; thank you for giving up life as you knew it when you were a twenty-two-year-old girl and becoming my mother and bringing me up for the last thirty-six years. Thanks, Mom, go on a cruise.

Then Marcia weighed in with her opinion and that about sewed it up.

"Take the cruise, Jill. Go. We're fine. There's no reason for you not to go. Lolo will be fine. What you gonna bring me? I want something from Greece."

We planned the trip. It was going to happen. We had a month to stabilize our little nursing home across the hall. Alison was around more, getting the feel of things, letting Jill see that she could handle it just fine.

The night before we flew off to Turkey, Joe and Teresa had us over for dinner. They wanted to say good-bye and had some things for us to take to Danila at the Palazzaccio—some beautiful photographs, portraits of Danila's daughter, Flavia, that Teresa had taken and printed. They were envious about our trip, and Joe cooked some Umbrian dishes to make us feel as if we were all over there together. Joe promised he would drop in on Lora regularly while we were gone and entertain her a bit.

After we got home, Jill went across the hall to say good night, and Lora grabbed her hand and wouldn't let it go. She waved away Kethleen, the night aide, and grabbed tightly onto Jill and glared at her in panic. Jill asked her if she wanted to come across to our apartment and Lora started walking immediately toward the door. Jill sat her down in our living room and tried to turn on the television; at that point we had three different remotes and she could never remember which one did what. She gave up. I was in bed already, helpful as always.

Jill sat there, holding her mother's hand, staring at nothing. She thought, "How can I leave her? She's defenseless and terrified. I'm her only lifeline. How can I even think of leaving her?"

Then she thought about her inner critic. This idea was from a book that her shrink had recommended. It's about how we all have an inner critic—Freud called it the superego —whose job it is to remind us what a piece of shit we are. And Jill thought back—just as the book told her to do—to when she first remembered feeling this way, back to when she was leaving for college and felt she was abandoning her mother. Even though Lora had wanted her to go away to school, had helped her choose the school, had taken her to visit campuses, Jill still felt that she was abandoning Lora and that Lora wouldn't survive without her.

She sat there and wept silently for a moment, as she always does when she finds the answer. She turned to her mom on the couch and said, "Ready to go back to your place?" And Lora nodded and docilely went back across the hall and went right to sleep. The next day we flew to Istanbul.

# TWENTY-SIX

# Away

I COULDN'T QUITE READ HER—Jill, that is. Probably because she didn't know herself how she felt. When the stewards sealed the door and the plane taxied to the runway, she looked over at me with a shrug that said, "Nothing I can do now; it's out of my hands." But whether that was a feeling of freedom or a feeling of hopelessness was hard to discern. Both, I imagine. So the trip would have to encompass both. I would have to honor her right to be anxious and then maybe she'd feel she had the space to have some fun.

"What are you thinking?"

"That my mother is asking where the hell I am. That she's furious at me for leaving her."

"I don't think that's what's happening. I don't think she even knows we live across the hall."

"Yeah, she does."

I didn't want to get into an argument, but every single time Lora came into our apartment, she was completely surprised that we lived there.

"What are you thinking about?" Jill asked.

"About tomorrow morning. We have a three-hour layover in the Vienna airport before we get on the plane for Istanbul."

"That's a drag."

"Yeah. Unless we want to go into town for a little while."

"Into Vienna?"

"Beats sitting in the airport."

"Do we have time?

"There's a train that goes right from the airport to the center of the historic section. They say it only takes twenty minutes. We could walk around, breathe some air, see the opera house, and then go to the Hotel Sacher for a piece of chocolate cake."

"Sacher torte?"

"Yeah. This is supposed to be the place."

"Wow."

That got her. Chocolate. One step at a time.

We hit the center of imperial Vienna at around 9:30 in the morning after at best three hours of sleep on the plane. Sleeping on a plane is a horrible thing to put yourself through, second only to not sleeping on the plane. And first class doesn't help all that much. Sorry, folks, but the biggest difference in first class is that when you wake up with a stiff neck, a headache, and no circulation in your legs, you're also $6,000 poorer.

It was a crisp, sunny morning and Vienna was dazzling. We walked around the famous Ring Road and saw the opera house and the imperial palace and all the monuments to the great composers. The Hotel Sacher was right across from the opera house. Built in the 1800s by Eduard Sacher, it soon became a meeting place for kings and prime ministers, the most elegant and important hotel in Vienna. Eduard was the son of Franz

Sacher, who as a sixteen-year-old baker's apprentice created a chocolate cake with apricot jam tucked under the chocolate frosting that became the talk of the town after it was served at a banquet for Prince von Metternich in 1832. The Hotel Sacher, a temple to Old World charm and elegance, was built around a slice of cake.

We were too late for breakfast and too early for lunch, so we had no problem being seated in the café. We ordered two slices of the cake, a Viennese coffee for me, and an herbal tea for Jill. We still had an hour to kill so we really took our time savoring the cake, which definitely lived up to its reputation. The coffee was the real deal, too, strong and fragrant, a little spicy. The early spring sunlight lit the street outside the window like a movie set. I lifted my cup to Jill and we clinked.

"Here's to getting away."

When we got to Istanbul, we were met at the airport and taken directly to the ship. By the time we got settled and unpacked, it was late in the afternoon and we decided to just stay on board and crash. We would explore Istanbul the next day after we got some sleep. Jill was able to put calls through to New York and spoke with Marcia and Alison. Everything was fine and dandy there. Marcia tried to put Lora on the phone, but that wasn't a good idea. Lora was essentially aphasic at this point; she could start a thought but couldn't really get past the first word or two. So Jill ended up trying to supply both sides of the conversation; over an international phone connection, this was an exercise in frustration.

The next day we met Michael Kuser for lunch. He's a journalist who lives and works in Istanbul, and he's the son of our friend George in Umbria. He took us to a restaurant with an outside terrace that overlooked the historical peninsula. During lunch we listened to the calls to prayer from the various mosques scattered around the city, most of them eerily amplified over a sound system. This was our first experience in the Orient, our first predominantly Muslim city, and with our jet lag, we both felt weirded out by how foreign everything was. Michael, who is married to a Turkish woman and had just fathered twins, told us a bit about what it was like to live in this city where East meets West. Then we went off on our own for a whirlwind peek at some of the highlights of this amazing town—the Blue Mosque, Topkapi Palace, Haghia Sophia, and the Grand Bazaar—and then hurried back to the ship to sail off at sunset.

The thing about a cruise is that it's just like cruising. You stop in at a bar, your eyes flick over to an interesting person sitting on one of the stools, you check out her most obvious attributes, and then your eyes move on to the next person. You're not looking to stay and have a meaningful conversation, you're not seeking a relationship, you're cruising. Every place our ship docked was worth more time, but all we could do was leave a bookmark and hope we could get back some day. There were two highlights worth mentioning, though: the first was when we docked at the Turkish town of Kusadasi and took a bus to the excavation at Ephesus, which is perhaps the largest, most intact archaeological site in the world. The city of Ephesus dates back to the tenth century B.C. By around 500 B.C. it was the most important seaport of the ancient word—the New York City of its time. But by the mid-400s after Christ, silt from the river had filled in the harbor and the city was abandoned, covered over, and eventually completely forgotten—except in myth. Then in the late 1800s an English archaeologist and engineer, J. T. Wood, uncovered part of the temple of Artemis and the dig began. At this point, they've uncovered only 15 percent of it, but it's a city that you can walk through, down broad avenues and past temples, a library, and an enormous amphitheater. We were transported; the sense of all that time passing took us out of ourselves. If a great city could disappear and be forgotten under centuries of sand, one grain at a time, then our problems—Lora, the aides, our kids, money—seemed quite manageable.

The second highlight was the day we landed on Italian soil at Taormina in Sicily. I know it sounds silly; we've lived in Italy for only five years, and neither of us is Italian by blood, but we all but ran down the gangplank and knelt and kissed the ground. We were home. People were speaking Italian! And we could understand them!

"*Buongiorno, buongiorno!*" we said to no one in particular as we walked through the Porta Messina, one of the gates of the old city, and made our way up the hill into town. "*Che bel giorno.*"

Taormina is a tourist town, for sure. All the shops, restaurants, and hotels are geared to serve the cruise ships and other tourists. But that didn't bother us on this particular morning. We were in Italy, and that was good. We stopped at a shop that sold handmade linens and bought a tablecloth for our outdoor table under the pergola. To be honest, we didn't need a tablecloth. We just wanted to have a conversation in Italian with someone. The woman in the shop was very nice and indulged us completely. We told her about our house in Umbria and she asked about where we lived in the states. Jill discussed the size of the table and which color tablecloth would go best with our dishes. We asked about her family and whether she had always lived in Taormina. We jabbered on until she finally told us how well we spoke Italian and how good our accents were. That was all we wanted to hear. We took our tablecloth and went to find the San Domenico Palace Hotel, which has beautiful gardens over-looking the ocean. We had been there on our first trip to Taormina a few years before, and Jill wanted to walk through the gardens again. The hotel was once a monastery dating back to 1400; now it's more like a museum with ancient frescoes, sculptures, and tapestries on display as you walk down the long corridors. We went outside and followed a path through the lush gardens, the bougainvillea draped around arbors, the blue Mediterranean below us; we sat on a bench and soaked up the sun, the fragrant air, the sea, and the flowers. We sat for a long time and said nothing. I knew Jill was thinking about her mom. She and Lora used to enjoy seeing flowers together, spending long afternoons at the arboretum in Santa Barbara. Jill was thinking how much her mom would appreciate this garden in Taormina—Lora would be able to name all the flowers. We sat there, letting time pass until Jill realized she was hungry—something I can always count on.

"Do you have a plan for lunch?" Jill asked.

"Does Howdy Doody have a wooden honker?"

We found a taxi that would take us up to Castelmola. Taormina is a hill town; Castelmola is on the hill above it. It's a tiny town, more like a neighborhood, with some good restaurants, some tourist shops, a great church and a 360-degree view of the ocean, Mount Etna (which was smoking away that day), and the Italian mainland at Reggio di Calabria. On the way up the hill—almost at the top—is a restaurant called Terrazza Auteri. It's cut into the side of the mountain with three levels of terraces, so that every table has the big view. We could see our cruise ship, which looked like a little toy boat in the distance.

We were on the early side of lunch, so the place was empty. Our waitress came with menus and we ordered some mineral water and a carafe of white wine. In the traditional Italian manner, she turned our glasses right side up to receive their various liquids, and this further reminded us that we were home. I started with *spaghetti alle vongole* and Jill just had a simple green salad as a first course. This goes a long way to explain why one of our stomachs is flat and the other round.

*Spaghetti alle vongole*—spaghetti with clam sauce—is a perfect example of why eating Italian food in Italy is a whole different experience from eating it anywhere else. I'm not saying you shouldn't eat Italian food in America; I'm just saying it's different in Italy. This can be chalked up to the freshness of the ingredients in Italy, the earth that the Italians grow things in, the air, the water—but most of all to the fact that the Italians have a thousand-year tradition of cooking things a certain way, and they know how to do it. With *spaghetti alle vongole,* for example, the trick is to let the clams open in the sauce so that their juices flavor it, then half-cook the spaghetti, throw it into the sauce—which is butter, wine, pancetta, garlic, onion, and the clam juice—and finish cooking it by letting the pasta suck up all these tastes into each strand of the spaghetti, much as the rice does in a risotto. Twirling some of this onto your fork and taking a sip of fresh, local white wine while gazing at the Mediterranean through the bougainvillea—what can I say?

The second course for each of us was a simple grilled fish. The waitress deboned the fish at the table and left us with a bottle of good olive oil (I recommend you forgo the squeeze of lemon and dribble some extra-virgin olive oil over it instead; lemon's a strong taste and masks the sweetness of the fish). Now, don't get me wrong—I like Greece and some of my best friends are Greek, but we had been eating grilled fish in every Greek port we stopped at for the past week and nothing tasted anywhere near as delicious as this. A simple piece of fish, simply grilled; same ocean—how could there be such a difference?

Our last stop before Rome was Naples—*bella Napoli*. A lot of people—a lot of Americans, especially—don't like Naples. It's too dirty, too congested, too chaotic, too much controlled by crime syndicates. I'm not one of those Americans; Naples takes my breath away. The cruise had a number of guided tours scheduled for the day in port—to the ruins of Pompeii and Herculaneum; to Positano, Sorrento, and the Amalfi coast; a museum tour of Naples itself. I put together a private shore excursion for a few couples we had befriended during the cruise, to walk through the teeming, tangled, chaotic mass of cars, buses, bicycles, mopeds, scooters, and pedestrians up the Corso Umberto 1, past the magnificent buildings of the University of Naples to the corner where the Corso, via Sersalle, and via Colletta come together. This is the home of Da Michele, which has been serving some of the best pizza in the world since the late 1800s.

Da Michele is pure. It serves only two kinds of pizza—with cheese and without. It sells water and beer. That's that. No sausage, no onion, no pepperoni. Nothing but a pure "margherita," which is with tomato sauce, mozzarella cheese—preferably from the milk of the southern Italian buffalo—and a little basil thrown on after the pie comes out of the oven; and a "marinara," a pizza with tomato sauce, garlic, and a little anchovy, but no cheese on top. No other options are available. I asked the waiter if I could have some hot pepper flakes to put on my pizza, and he looked at me as if I had offended his mother. If you want something else on your pizza or a glass of wine with your lunch, go across the street to Trianon, which also has phenomenal pizza but is less pure. Either way, you can't miss. Our friends from the cruise had a great time. We had given them a real Italian experience, not the typical guided tour through the time-tested tourist attractions that the cruise line usually offers. The walk from the pier to Da Michele, through the chaos that is Naples, carried with it a sense of danger and adventure and gave them an authentic taste of this amazing city.

The last night on board ship, the purser asked us if we wanted him to arrange a car or limo to meet us at the pier at Civitavecchia, the port of Rome. We explained that we had already arranged to be met by Alessandra, the woman who runs our video rental shop in Spoleto. He shot us the same look the waiter had given me at Da Michele.

## TWENTY-SEVEN

# Home

ALESSANDRA IS MANY THINGS—a mother, a driver, a video-store operator—but above all, she is an Italian. This means that she was forty-five minutes late to pick us up at the pier. We didn't mind too much. We watched all the more well-heeled types debark, with their chauffeurs hoisting expensive luggage into the trunks of Mercedes limos, until Alessandra's slightly battered Toyota pulled in to pick us up. It felt right. We were, after all, the entertainment.

Jill sat up front with Alessandra on the drive home and they immediately got down to basics: How's your mother? How's your son? Alessandra told us about putting him in a new school program for children with special needs, so that he was able to enjoy his time there more. We've learned a lot about the pluses and minuses of the Italian health care system from talking to Alessandra about her son. Although the government pays for everything in Italy, Italians don't have as many options for care as we do in the states. But she was, as always, upbeat about his progress.

Then it was Jill's turn to vent all her feelings about her mom's situation to a very sympathetic ear. And because she had to do it in Italian, everything had to be rethought. Some-times words lose their meaning when we use them over and over, and having to search for Italian words and phrases to describe her feelings to Alessandra forced Jill to look at the whole situation with fresh eyes. By the time we turned onto the dirt road that leads down to our house, Jill was calmer than I had seen her in months. It was as if she'd had a therapy session.

"Do you see those women by the side of the road?" asked Alessandra. "They're gathering the wild asparagus. You came at a good time of year."

This got me very excited. We had tons of asparagus on our property every spring—hidden in the high grass all around the olive trees. When we first bought the house, Bruno pointed it out to us and taught us how to find it. It wasn't easy because the stalks—much thinner and darker green than the cultivated variety we know in the states—are camouflaged by the wild grasses that they hide among. You have to train your eye to see them.

After I lugged the suitcases upstairs for Jill to unpack, I set out to the meadow to hunt down the wild asparagus. I perched myself on the low stone wall next to our vegetable garden, which was lying fallow after the winter, and took a few deep breaths. Hunting asparagus is like meditation—one has to be calm and quiet or the stalks won't reveal themselves. I blurred my vision a little so that I wasn't looking directly at them; this is a good way to fool them into appearing. While I waited, I thought about what I would do with them when I caught them; a little pasta—maybe penne—with some bits of Ugo's prosciutto and the cut-up asparagus in a sauce of but-ter, a touch of cream, parmigiano, and a grating of pepper. Yeah, that would do it. All I needed now was to find some of the little fuckers. In truth, I have never found any asparagus. Bruno—standing right next to me—found handfuls of them; Jill had no difficulty spotting them; but for some reason, they have never deigned to reveal themselves to me. Probably this is some form of anti-Semitism.

"Mike!" Jill was calling from the bedroom upstairs.

"Honey, I'm in the middle of hunting asparagus. You're spooking them."

"We don't have any water."

"What?"

"There's no water."

"Try the bathroom sink."

When she didn't reply, I realized that she had probably already tried the bathroom sink, and that this was how she found out that there was no water in the first place. I left my perch with the score one to nothing, favor of asparagus, and went to see what was going on.

Indeed there was no water. In the kitchen I flipped the handle on the faucet and a tiny breath of air came out, then nothing. I flipped it again as I had been taught to do at the Harvard Graduate School of Plumbing, but still nothing but air. I would have to call a gentile.

"Call Martin."

I knew that. I picked up the phone to dial our architect and friend, who lives up the hill, and in the receiver I heard a sound not unlike the one made by the kitchen faucet—an airy, empty, forlorn sound—a sound of dysfunction and despair.

"The phone's dead."

Jill came slowly down the stairs to join me and we stood there in silence, looking at the dead phone. All the excitement of our arrival, the romance of a house in Umbria, the freedom of escaping the complexities of our life back in the states—all lay in a shambles at our feet. We're actors; we know when the scene's not working.

"Where's the *telefonino*?"

That's what the Italians call their cell phones. I had it in my carry-on bag with the luggage. I called Martin, but all I got was the recorded voice of Telecom, a woman explaining that the party I dialed was either busy or away from the phone or having lunch.

I tried Sophie, our landscaper and friend. She actually answered.

"Hey, Soph, we're here!"

"Great. *Bentornati*."

"Well, great and not so great. We have no water."

"Oh, yeah, I heard they're fixing a pipe or something. It's been off for a couple of days in your area. But don't worry, I've been over to check the geraniums and they'll be fine."

"Well, I wasn't thinking about the geraniums, actually. We just got off the road and we were looking forward to a shower. And cooking is going to be a problem, too."

"You can shower at our place, if you want."

Her place was a twenty-minute drive. And anyway, we didn't want a shower at her place. We wanted to shower in our own beautiful bathroom that we had built at great personal expense.

"Is Elias around?" Elias is her son and the local computer and electronics genius.

"Yeah, I think I can find him. Why?"

"Our landline is out, too—which also means we can't check our e-mail. We need to be in touch for all kinds of reasons—Jill's mom can't hear well on the cell phone and Jill needs to be able to speak with her. "

She said she'd send Elias over right away and we made plans to have dinner that night at the Palazzaccio. Almost immediately, the *telefonino* rang again. It was Martin.

"You're here! Finally!" he said, warmly.

"Yeah, but we have no water."

"Oh, I know, I know. We had the same problem last week. It's a real pain. If you want, you can shower at our place until it comes back on."

We thanked him and asked if he and Karen could join us at the Palazzaccio for dinner. Then Jill and I sat at the table outside under the pergola and attempted to regroup.

"Here's the way I see it." I had her hand in mine and I was stroking her arm. It was my job to make this all better, which is what husbands are for.

"We have to start with what is, honey—not with how we want things to be. We thought we were coming here to relax, to eat and drink and play with our pals; we thought we were coming here to regenerate ourselves, detoxify ourselves, rediscover each other."

She nodded, a little moisture welling up in her eyes.

"But now we realize that what we're actually here for is to get the water turned back on and to argue with the fucking phone company. That's what the universe is telling us."

She usually likes this universe stuff, but this time she looked at me as if I had just passed wind.

"That doesn't make me feel better," she said drily.

I was about to further my philosophical point when we heard the sound of a motor scooter coming down the road. It was Elias, coming to do battle with Telecom.

"We'll get back to this." I was feeling defensive and a little incompetent—as if my ability to husband her was on a par with my plumbing expertise. We went over to greet Elias, who was taking off his helmet.

"I hear your water's off."

We nodded. He shrugged.

"You can take a shower at our place."

In the off-season—especially in the middle of the week—the Palazzaccio is a completely different animal. In the summer, throngs of people are eating outside at long picnic tables and a table-hopping party atmosphere prevails; but now, in the early spring with the chill of winter still hovering, only a few tables are set inside, usually in the front room around the fireplace, which is the main source of heat other than the kitchen. Often the only diners are the husbands of Danila, Teresa, and Nicla, who run the place. The guys will drive in to spend the evening with their wives and sip grappa and argue politics after dinner; maybe they'll bring the kids to do their homework by the fire.

A table was set up for us right in front of the fireplace. Martin, Karen, Sophie, and Jeffrey came out for our welcome-home dinner. Bruno and Mayes were in Rome visiting Bruno's mother and would be back the next day. And that was about it. The rest of our little expat community was either back at work in the states or headed off for some warm place. JoJo and Bruce were still in Vietnam. They'd be back home for the summer.

Danila brought out some bruschetta topped with a paste made from a mixture of wild mushrooms and the precious winter truffles that grow around the local oak trees. The summer truffles, which won't be available until mid-July, are less pungent—and much less expensive—but they are plentiful and the Palazzaccio has an entire separate menu with dishes that feature *tartufi*.

We were feeling better. Our water had come back on in time for us to shower before coming to dinner. The telephone, however, was a different story. The problem—as well as Elias could interpret it from his conversation with Telecom—was that we had missed paying a bill over a year before. It must have fallen through the crack when we shifted from having JoJo pay our bills to having them paid through the bank. One bill got lost in the shuffle. And Telecom, in its infinite wisdom, never carried that balance over to the subsequent bills—all of which we've paid diligently and on time. Telecom just waited a year without saying anything and then cut off our service. And it wasn't going to be easy to get it turned back on. One solace was that we weren't alone; everybody at the table had a story about Telecom.

"We had a loose cable coming into the house and I called them to send someone out," said Sophie. "But in my frustration, I spoke to the lady in the familiar rather than the formal—the *tu* as opposed to the *lei*—and she had our service cut off. I couldn't believe it."

"So what do we do?" Jill asked.

"Use your cell phone," said Jeffrey.

"They have a monopoly," said Martin. "They can do what they please."

The *primi* came out and the wine pitchers were refilled. I had the tortellini in cream sauce with bits of sausage and Jill had arugula salad with parmigiano shaved over it. Danila suggested that maybe a local might have more luck with Telecom than a foreigner.

"You should have Vittoria call them," said Karen. "She's amazing with things like that."

"No one dares to say no to Vittoria," added Martin.

This was true. Vittoria is much more than a cleaning woman. She went to war over our electric bill for us the year before and won a great victory. When she finally got the man from ENEL, the electric company, to come to the house, she proved to him that no one had been living there—we had been in the states for nine months—and that the meter must be faulty. She's only five feet tall but she backed the man into a corner and wouldn't let him out until he capitulated. Our electric bill has been very reasonable ever since.

After dinner, when Danila brought the grappa bottle over, her husband, Vezio, joined us. After a few glasses of grappa, Vezio loves to practice his English and talk about American films, of which he has an encyclopedic knowledge. In his youth, Vezio was a karate expert—a world champion in his weight class. Then, after a knee injury he changed sports and became a very successful professional boxer. He still keeps himself in great shape. Danila came and sat down—after bringing out a few pieces of *torta di ricotta,* a warm cheesecake with blackberry jam on top, for the table to share. We gave her the photos that Teresa had sent from New York of their daughter, Flavia, and everyone cooed over them. Jeffrey showed us photos of his newest pieces—four enormous oil paintings with strong political overtones. This, of course, led us into a discussion of politics, both American and Italian. Danila and Vezio are more on the conservative side of things; the rest of us are flagrant liberals. A very emotional conversation ensued about Bush and Berlusconi. Voices were raised; the grappa flowed. We were home.

# TWENTY-EIGHT

# Pettino

IT TOOK US ABOUT A WEEK TO TRULY BE THERE, to actually achieve "Italian." Karen would drive down the hill in the morning, and she and Jill did an hour and a half of yoga together while I made coffee and did some writing. Then I would go into town to reestablish contact with my food providers. First I stopped at Ugo's to lay in a *guanciale,* some house-made prosciutto, and a wheel of pecorino cheese that Ugo gets from a real shepherd he knows who has real sheep that live on a real hillside up the mountain. Then I would buy something to make for dinner—pork chops or a boned leg of lamb or some ribs to grill over the fire. But also I went to Ugo for some conversation in the local dialect—both with the man himself and with the women in line in front of me. They asked what I was making, and when I told them the recipe, they corrected me and told me exactly how they would do it. There's no better Italian lesson.

Then I went to our little bakery to get Jill some *integrale*— whole wheat bread that just came out of the oven—and then I popped across the street to Sabrina's *alimentari* for some yogurt and whatever fruit was in season. After her yoga and meditation, Jill likes to make toast for breakfast, drizzle some olive oil over it, and then add a slice of the cheese from Ugo. After that, she tucks into a bowl of the yogurt with fruit. Breakfast takes up most of the rest of the morning.

Domenico came by around eleven with our Christmas present—four months late, but time wasn't really the issue. He had six five-liter cans of olive oil for us. It was the yearly yield from our olive trees, harvested in November and taken to the *cooperativo* to be pressed. It would keep us in oil for the rest of the year. Not just oil, but our oil—which just happens to be the best olive oil in the world. We promised him that next year we would be here to pick the olives ourselves—or at least help him with the picking. Then we spent an hour or so with him planning the *orto* so that it would be ready to feed us when we came back in the summer. We'd have tomatoes, zucchini, eggplant, green beans, peppers—both sweet and hot—celery, lots of types of lettuces, and arugula. Domenico calls the lettuce area *insalata per Gille*—Jill's salad.

Bruno and Mayes were back from Rome and asked us if we wanted to go with them to Pettino for lunch the next day. Pettino is a tiny town all the way up the mountain behind our house. It has a few houses, a lot of farms carved into the sloping hillsides, and clear views of the snow-covered Sibillini, which are part of the Apennine mountain chain that extends the entire length of the Italian peninsula. The Sibillini mountains are named after the ancient soothsayer who is said to have lived in a cave on what now is Monte Sibilla.

In Pettino there's a little inn with a restaurant that, as far as I can tell, is the only commercial building in town. Bruno and Mayes know the owners and they wanted us to meet this family. They came to the Rustico a little early because they love the house—especially Mayes, who secretly still thinks of it as hers. Before they sold it to us, when they owned it and lived in it, they planted the fruit trees—the plum, nectarine, and almond trees that give us so much pleasure in the summer and fall. Bruno also planted seventy-five young olive trees to supplement the mature trees that have been growing around the house, giving fruit for centuries. Mayes first planted the vegetable garden that we've taken over with the help of Domenico. And Bruno, of course, was responsible for modernizing the old cottage while still keeping its 350-year-old character intact. So, they have a lot of themselves in the house.

"Wow, the *gelso* is in good shape," said Bruno as he walked up the front steps. "What have you been feeding this guy?"

A *gelso* is a mulberry tree, and ours is a beauty that sits in the ell we created when we added the new wing onto the house. The tree is the focal point of the house, framing the entrance and rising up above the second-floor windows. It was having some health problems when Bruno and Mayes lived in the house, and they saved it by calling in a tree surgeon who hollowed all the diseased areas out of the trunk. This created a kind of ledge, which you can sit on—or rather in—like a throne built into the tree. When we took over the stewardship, Sophie advised us to let Domenico cut the branches back rather severely each year in the fall, and this did the trick. They grew back every spring with full, lush leaves that create a canopy over our entranceway all through the summer.

"It's our protector. It guards the house," I said to Bruno.

"Yeah, it's a great old guy." You could tell the tree meant a lot to him.

We piled into our car and headed up the mountain. Our house stands at about twelve hundred feet—four hundred meters—above sea level. Pettino is about a thousand meters above that. We drove past Lenano; we drove past Campello Alto, which is a walled castle that protected our hillsides in the Middle Ages; we passed Fontanelle, which has a lovely restaurant of its own; and we climbed up to where the road has striped poles along the side to measure the snowfall. Then we reached Pettino. At that altitude, there were no wildflowers covering the hillsides yet; in Pettino, spring was still a few weeks away.

We parked the car at the bottom of the driveway and hiked up the long stairway to the restaurant. We were met at the top by signor Marsiglia, the *padrone* of the family, who looked as if he had just gotten back from hunting. He wore one of those jackets with all the pockets that hunters use to carry their ammunition and things. But instead, his pockets were filled with black truffles that—with the help of his trusty dog—he had just foraged from under the oaks on the hillside. He winked at Bruno to indicate that we would be tasting one of these beauties shortly after we sat down at the table.

We sat by the fire, and one of the daughters brought out plates of bruschetta topped with truffle paste, along with pitchers of water and wine. Mamma was hidden away in the kitchen doing her magic with the pots and pans. Then we all had the house specialty, which is a hand-rolled pasta—much like the *strozzapreti* (priest stranglers) that you see in Tuscany. These come in a creamy sauce, lightly sweetened with tomato and then showered with more fresh truffle shavings than you would think would be economically feasible. This dish would be worth walking the fourteen kilometers up the mountain from our house. Then Jill had an omelet for her *secondo*. This is a classic Umbrian dish and a perfect example of Italian cooking at its best. The ingredients—eggs, fresh from the henhouse right outside the door; shaved truffles that we had seen in the *padrone*'s pocket moments before; and salt and pepper. That's it. You can't eat better food than this.

The rest of us had thin lamb chops, which were also very local. I'm sure they had just been home-butchered from one of those cute little woolly things we saw dotting the hillsides outside, then pounded thin and quickly grilled over wood. They went down very nicely with what tasted to me like homemade wine. It is called *genuino* in these parts—the best translation would be "moonshine"—and it's made in the bathtub or a big old pot. Sometimes it's good; at other times it can taste like lighter fluid. This version was made by pros and was quite good.

We stayed and talked with the family after we finished eating. Dessert was a nutty, winy cake that Mamma made—not too sweet and perfect with a glass of Vin Santo. Every moment around the table further served to loosen our shoulders and clear away the storm inside our heads. We were away and we were home—a nice combination.

That evening we hunkered down at the house and did nothing. It felt like heaven. I built a fire and we snacked on some leftovers. We were pretty much sated from lunch. Jill called New York on our cell phone—as she did every night—and everything was calm and running smoothly. Occasionally she tried to speak with Lora, but it was never easy; sometimes Lora called her Lois, who is Lora's older sister. When Jill said, "I love you" at the end of the phone call, Lora repeated it back to her, and this made Jill happy. In her mind, she was still half in New York, but the half that was in Umbria was feeling the spaciousness that she had been craving. After the phone call, we sat by the fire and talked about how she was feeling. I mostly just listened and let her get her thoughts and worries off her chest. The more she was able to vent, the more present she seemed to be with me. So the weeks in Italy turned into a very intimate time between us.

We went to a dinner party at AP&P's house. That's Bruno's name for Anna Paola and Paolo, who have become good friends of ours through Bruno and Mayes. They live just outside Trevi, a beautiful hill town just north of us. These evenings are special to us because they're in Italian; no English is spoken. Anna Paola is a teacher and an actress, and Paolo is a mosaicist and jewelry maker. We have one of his beautiful mosaic tile tables in our living room. Also at dinner was Giancarlo, an old friend of Bruno and Mayes, who is a famous designer for theater and opera. We talked on into the night about theater and various productions we'd been involved in or seen. Theater is an international language, it seems, so we had no problem following and participating in the conversation. By the time we got home that night, we found ourselves speaking to each other in Italian, thinking in Italian, and, finally, dreaming in Italian.

Another day, we walked over to the Villa Della Genga, which is just down the road and around the hill from us. It's a fantastic property that's been in the same family since the fifteenth century. The main building was a hunting lodge for Pope Leo XII, the della Genga pope who is buried in the cathedral in Spoleto. These days, the Montani family is using the estate to produce high-quality organic olive oil and organic grains and legumes. They've also converted some of the smaller buildings into *casette* that they rent out, and they have another set of buildings down the road that they've turned into a small bed-and-breakfast and conference center. Everything they've done is first-rate and in beautiful taste, and their oil is among the finest in the area. Paolo Montani is a direct descendant of the della Genga clan and he's now a businessman who spends the week working in Rome and then comes home for the weekends to join his wife, Alessandra. She and their son, Filippo, oversee the business.

We first met Alessandra a couple of years before, when we wandered over there to see what they were doing and to taste their oil. When she realized we were neighbors, she invited us to dinner that night. It was a casual affair, with Alessandra cooking in their fifteenth-century kitchen. It started with an appetizer of fried stuffed zucchini blossoms and fried sage leaves in the lightest batter I have ever tasted.

"It's a simple recipe," said Alessandra. "Everything is one."

When she saw my puzzled face, she clarified:

"*Un cucchiaio d'olio* (one tablespoon of oil).

"*Un cucchiaio di grappa* (the same amount of grappa).

"*Cento grammi di farna* (one hundred grams of flour).

"*Acqua per l'ochio* (water 'to the eye')—in other words, add enough water to the mixture so that it becomes a batter that's not too thick, not too thin.

"*E un po' di sale. E basta.* A little salt and that's it."

Try it, it's the lightest batter going—must be the grappa.

That day we found Alessandra in the garden and asked her if she wanted to have dinner that night. She's often alone during the week and appreciates company. We decided no one would cook and we'd try a new trattoria that had opened down on the Flaminia next to the Fonti. That night there was a cool spring shower and we were the only ones in the restaurant. We cozied up around the fire, had a simple meal, and gossiped on into the night. Another Italian evening with only a minimum of English.

Two days before we left to go back to New York, we were talking to Alison on the phone. Everything was fine on the mother front, but we could tell that Alison was ready to get out from under having responsibility for Lora.

"I'm definitely ready for you guys to come home," she told us.

"Two days and we'll be there to take over."

"It's not that, really. I think I just miss you."

## TWENTY-NINE

# Open Eyes

JILL'S EPIPHANY WAS SO SUBTLE it was barely perceptible to anyone but herself. We walked into Lora's apartment after we dropped our suitcases across the hall, and Lora looked up at her with a surprised and pleased look as if to say, "What are *you* doing here?" And Jill knew that she hadn't been missed, that she hadn't been in Lora's thoughts when we were away—except perhaps for the few confusing moments when they tried to speak on the phone. Jill tensed for a rebuke, a look of recrimination, but there was none. Lora didn't know we had been away; she didn't know we lived across the hall. She was delighted to see Jill and she'd be sorry to see her walk out the door, as she would be the next morning and the next. Most of the time she thought Jill was her older sister, Lois, and that they were girls together. Who the hell she thought I was in this whole scenario I have no idea, but she was always happy to see me, too.

Later that night when we finally, exhaustedly, fell into bed, Jill told me that besides feeling little explosions of relief—freedom bombs going off inside her—she also had the sense that she had lost something. I understood the sense of loss because of a similar experience I had with my mother. My certifiable, certified-borderline-personality-disorder mom, who had been such an attractive and destructive figure in my life, just upped and vanished on me one day in 1986. She was visiting us in Los Angeles just after *L.A. Law* had gone on the air. I was suddenly famous—television famous—and my mother was oddly cowed by that. She treated me like a guest on the Letterman show, like an icon who had to be catered to. And I felt abandoned. Where was my mom? My cruelly honest mother who deftly dealt me the ego-deflating card whenever I was feeling too full of myself? "C'mon, Mom. Hit me hard and low like only you can." But she couldn't let herself do that any more, not to someone who was on television. And I felt that I had lost my mother.

Jill had been playing the role of her mother's protector, her apologist, and her translator to the world for so long that now, when Lora was obviously beyond keeping up appearances, Jill felt orphaned. Jill had been running interference all these years, and now she was out of a job. The irony, of course, was that not until her mother fell into dementia and actually, physically needed care was Jill able to extricate herself from her lifelong role of caretaker.

And the freedom part? For Jill, freedom came over time, in little steps. Over the next few months, she kept trying it on like a new outfit, checking it out in the mirror from all angles, and then putting it back in the closet. We took a weekend trip to a friend's house in the country and she commented on how much "lighter" she felt, getting away from her mom.

"I keep waiting for the ax to fall and when it doesn't I'm always surprised. It's like Pavlov's dog—I'm waiting to feel the guilt descend on me because I'm doing something for myself, and each time it doesn't happen, I feel a little more free."

She came home one day from her singing teacher all lit up, telling me about a breakthrough.

"My God, this sound came out of me today that I've never heard before. It was like hearing my own voice for the first time."

Little by little, her attitude toward her mom turned from one of guilt and responsibility to one of real warmth. She came back across the hall one day after spending some time with Lora and had another breakthrough to tell me about.

"I'm starting to feel completely unconflicted about being affectionate with her—a lot because I'm not worried about her response. It may be reciprocated or not—I don't feel it's about her response any more. It just feels good to feel affection for her. It's not conditional. That's a first for me."

Lora, for her part, had become fat and happy—literally. She found Alison's cooking irresistible. Actually, Lora had always had a good appetite, she was just waiting for some food that was worth eating. She put back all the weight she had lost since Ralph died and a bit more. Jill had to let out some of her pants, and we shopped for things that had spandex in the waistbands. Her moods were downright jolly most of the time, and jolly is not a term that had heretofore ever been attributed to Lora. Letting go of any pretense was a huge relief for her. After all those years of pretending to be able to hear, pretending to be an intellectual equal in every conversation—letting all that go made her . . . well, jolly.

It was as Josie had said to us when she was trying to sell us on the dementia ward in Santa Barbara. "These people are happy," she said. "They've let it go. There's a real calm in that." We couldn't see it then, but it was true.

The other big factor was the absence of drugs in her system. With the doctor's supervision and approval, Marcia removed her from all the antidepressants, antipsychotics, sleeping pills—all that stuff. And Lora's doctor, after testing, decided she could do without her heart medicine as well. Without a doubt, Lora was happier for this, more alert and energetic.

Even though I was a lesser participant in Lora's social life—I had to continually remind everyone that I needed my privacy and that our apartment had to be sacrosanct—I did manage to have some fun times with her. We had a shared passion—televised golf. Sometimes we'd watch at her apartment; sometimes I'd get her to come over to my place. We both liked to doze. We'd watch the ball go up, then we'd watch it come down, then it went plop, plop, plop onto the green and we were out. Golf is very calming—especially if the couch is comfortable. Lora liked to chortle when somebody missed a putt, and I thought at first this showed a sadistic side I hadn't known about. But then she chortled when somebody made the putt as well. She just thought the whole thing was a stitch.

Joe, her regular beau, came over to visit whenever he could. One night he and Teresa were at our place for an easy dinner—some *bucatini all'amatriciana* made with the guanciale that I smuggled back from our last trip to Italy, and a simple salad—and while the rest of us were cleaning up, Joe went across the hall to spend some time with Lora. A while later, when he didn't come back, Jill went over to see what happened and found them side by side on the couch fast asleep with the television showing an old *Reba* rerun. Those crazy kids.

We fired the weekend aide. Jill had been hesitant to let her go because even though she was a pain in the ass, Lora knew her face and had gotten used to her. Change was the big enemy for Lora. But after much discussion—with me, with

Marcia, with her therapist—Jill realized that she had to replace the weekend aide for her own peace of mind. So finally she did. And into the space came Buela, who has been a godsend. Buela is a calm and deeply loving person. She will sit for hours on the couch next to Lora, holding her hand or gently stroking her arm. Lora has a tiny stuffed puppy that she loves to hold, and Buela will pat the puppy and coo to it and Lora will look on with approval. When Lora speaks—or tries to speak—Buela looks directly into her eyes and receives the communication. Buela is very Zen.

Marcia, on the other hand, is more like Lora's mate. They bicker like two old married people. Every morning, Marcia will cajole Lora out of bed to get washed up and dressed. Lora hates to get up and gives Marcia a lot of resistance—often taking a swing at her, which sends Marcia into roaring laughter. Marcia always manages to win. And she always does it in such a way that Lora thinks she's the winner. They laugh a lot; they make bets.

"I'll bet you that once you get outside, you goin' to be very happy to be out there. You'll see."

"Oh, yeah?" says Lora pugnaciously. *You and who else?* is implied in her tone.

"You'll see, Lolo," Marcia says in a singsong, like an eight-year-old on the playground. "When you get out there you'll see that I'm right." And she throws her head back and laughs.

Their morning routine can take hours, with Marcia cajoling and wagering and mock-threatening Lora through her breakfast. Then they'll get her all bundled up, even when it's warm outside; Lora hates to be cold. And they'll take the wheelchair down in the elevator and Marcia will make Lora push it all the way down the street to the park. Lora will complain that she's being tortured and abused and she'll try to sit down in the chair to be pushed, and Marcia will stand her up and make her push it farther.

"It's her exercise. She needs to walk and breathe some air and get her blood movin'. Otherwise she just gonna waste away."

I think she's right. Lora will probably live to be a hundred, after which Jill and I will be old enough to need Marcia. She can just move across the hall and take care of us.

Some days, Marcia will take Lora on the number five bus that goes all the way down to Lower Manhattan. The trip takes all day. They'll get off and watch the ferryboats or the children playing in Battery Park. They'll have a picnic. On the bus, Lora will read every sign she sees out the window and she'll mouth the words to herself. She's a big reader. Sometimes they won't get home until evening.

Kethleen, Lora's nighttime aide, completes the circle. She's the rock—solid as can be. Her main job is getting Lora cleaned up and ready for bed, which, depending on the mood of the moment, can be a tough job. But Kethleen is inexorable. She's calm and certain, and she makes Lora feel safe.

Our little family, which had come together this year like a nice Italian minestrone, was completed with the arrival of Dexter, Alison's dog, our granddog, Max's half brother.

Alison was having serious second thoughts about having left Dexter in Los Angeles. She missed him terribly. But she didn't think it was fair to her friend Shannon, who had adopted Dexter, to change her mind and take him back. She started looking around for another dog in New York to take his place. Then Shannon called Alison and they had a long and serious talk about what would be best for Dexter and finally decided that he should be returned to his real mom—well, to Alison, who started making plans for Dexter's trip to New York. She found a Web site where independent truckers advertised that, for a fee, they would transport pets. Alison interviewed a number of them over the phone until she found a guy she thought sounded responsible.

The trip across country took over a week. Every day Alison got an e-mail with a photo: here's Dexter relieving himself on a cactus, here's Dexter having the remains of a cheeseburger, here's Dexter and I at the Day's Inn in Minnesota, etcetera.

By the time they arrived in New York, the trucker and Dexter had bonded and the guy actually had tears in his eyes when he said good-bye. But that's Dexter. He has a way of squirreling himself into your heart.

He moved in with Alison and Max and immediately began to put his stamp on the household. Max would get home after a gig—often in the small hours of the morning—and Dexter would greet him at the door. After a moment of filial bonding, Max would take him out for a long walk and then feed him some doggy treats before they both went to bed. Whenever Alison was busy doing a catering job, Max would be responsible for Dexter, making sure he was fed and walked and properly cuddled. This was really Max's first experience of being responsible for another being, and, if I may say so, it actually helped boost him along into maturity. Good dog, Dexter!

For us, Dexter is the grandchild we feared we'd never have. When Alison cooks for her grandmother in our apartment, she walks Dexter down from her place through Riverside Park and leaves him with us while she goes shopping. Dexter, we feel, needs the attention and love that only a grandparent can give, so we spoil him thoroughly. The love fest starts the moment he comes through the door—well, after that tricky transition period when he jumps up and plants both his feet squarely into my private parts. Once we get past that, we're able to get to the love fest.

Jill's relationship with him is more maternal, of course: gentler, more nurturing. Mine tends to be more masculine in nature—some roughhousing, and then we'll have a pizza and some beer and fall asleep in front of the television with the football game on.

I can tell you this: I know love—from many, many years of experience in many different relationships—and this dog is crazy about me. This is the real thing. I can tell.

We tried to bring Dexter together with Lora, but his energy was a bit too much for her. She has her stuffed dog, of whom she is very fond, and it seems to be the right speed for her. One day, I was bringing Dexter back home from a walk in the park and we ran into Lora and Marcia. Lora was in her wheelchair and had her stuffed puppy cuddled right up next to her chin. She eyed Dexter warily and I bent down to her hearing aid and said, "My dog's bigger than your dog."

She thought that was pretty funny.

## THIRTY

# Life

THE PHONE RANG AGAIN. The York Theater on Lexington Avenue was producing a staged reading of a musical version of the play *Enter Laughing* and the director wanted to know if Jill and I would like to play the parents. We would rehearse the whole thing in five days and then perform it, scripts in hand, over the weekend. We'd open on Friday night, we'd have two shows on Saturday and two on Sunday, and that was it. We thought it would be fun to be involved with a musical—especially with such a short commitment—so we agreed.

Jill's a real singer. Years before she played the title role in a Broadway musical, *Onward Victoria,* which had the dubious distinction of closing on opening night. Its poster is on the wall at Joe Allen's, the famous theater bar and restaurant on Forty-sixth Street, whose walls are covered with posters of famous Broadway flops. Jill likes to sit at the table right beneath her poster whenever we eat there. It makes her feel like a Broadway legend.

I'm not a real singer. I have no posters at Joe Allen's. I've croaked my way through a few musical roles and gotten away with it because I was playing character parts, but no one has ever mistaken me for Ezio Pinza. This turned out to be fine, because when we got to our first rehearsal for *Enter Laughing* I found out that the father had no songs of his own. My only singing would be in the chorus numbers. On the one hand, I was relieved that I wouldn't have to worry about keeping up with the pro singers. On the other, it felt kind of dumb to be in a musical and not have a song to sing.

It was a whirlwind eight days, furiously rehearsing, learning the music, and figuring out how to carry a script and perform at the same time. Frankly, it felt like a total disaster until we opened and played our first performance, which turned out to be quite successful. All five shows were completely sold out and our friends who came to see the production raved about how good it was. The cast was wonderful—mostly young, deeply gifted actor-singer-dancers who were dazzling performers. We were the old people. Playing the Jewish father was not a stretch for me, but Jill's performance as the mother was a work of art. She deftly avoided the stereotypical Jewish mother and found the human, loving, doting woman beneath. Her two songs—"My Son, the Druggist" and "If You Want to Break Your Mother's Heart"—brought the house down.

Every night, we'd meet friends in the lobby after the show and go out to P. J. Clarke's, a venerable bar that was just around the corner from the theater. This is my favorite part of being an actor—going out for drinks after the show. The rest of it, frankly, you can have. You have to spend the whole day gearing up for the show, pampering yourself and protecting your voice—as if my voice were a national treasure. I can't eat before a show, so I nibble a little salad or something in the afternoon and that's it. There's not a moment in the day when I don't have some tension and anxiety about the performance that night.

But afterward is a real high. You've just come offstage from the curtain call, where many people have been applauding you. Invariably there's someone you know in the audience who comes backstage and gives you more praise. And then you go out and eat and drink and let all the tension of the day and the performance drain away. It's not half bad.

It was also fun to watch Jill get to shine and show off her talent. It was like watching her come back to life after a long illness. She thrives when she can express herself as the artist she is, and she craves being in the spotlight, garnering praise. And if she ever tells you different, don't believe her.

When we'd finally get home after the show and the carousing, she'd go over to her mom's apartment and say good night. Lora had always been a night owl and Jill would find her watching television in her pj's with Kethleen trying to coax her to bed. Jill would hold her hand for a while and then kiss her good night and tell her she loved her. Sometimes Lora would be able to say it back to her. These late-night look-ins were probably the most normal, healthy, unfettered time the two of them ever had together.

"Love you, Mom."

"Love you, too, Lois."

Well, you can't have everything.


We started to plan for our summer in Italy. Jill now had very little tension about the idea of getting away. The aides were up to speed, Alison and Max would look in and make sure everything was going smoothly, and there was really no reason for us not to go and rekindle our retirement dream. We were looking at being in Italy from the second week of July through August and into September, when the garden would be bursting with fresh produce, the festivals would be in full swing, and the full cast of characters would be there and ready to play.

We asked Alison if she could break away from her schedule and come over for a while. We felt Marcia and her crew could handle anything that came up with Lora and that Alison deserved a vacation. She jumped at the offer.

"I could fly over with you if that's okay. July is a slow time for me anyway. I have to be back to do a party on the twenty-fifth, so . . . maybe ten days?"

"Perfect."

Then Max asked if he and his new girlfriend, Marybeth—of whom we are very fond—could come over for a while. Because of their schedules—his gigs and her work as an editor for a publishing house—they could get away only for the first ten days of July.

"We're not getting there until the tenth," I told him. "You'll just miss us."

Max smothered a smile. "We'll manage," he said.

Obviously he hadn't been planning this as a trip with the parents. He wanted to be on his own there with Marybeth. He wanted to show her his house in Italy. He was also planning on having full use of the car.

"Well, Bruce and JoJo will be in the house for a couple of days. Is that okay? There's plenty of room."

They were back from their year in Vietnam but they couldn't get into their own house until their renters vacated on July 3.

"They'll be staying in the bedroom in the old part of the house, so you'll still have plenty of privacy."

"Sure, I love those guys," said Max. He and their son, Miles, had shared an apartment in New York, and he knew them quite well. And Bruce and JoJo could help orient the kids for a couple of days and then leave them to have their own adventures.

Well, okay. It would actually work out better if Alison and Max weren't there at the same time—so that one of them could be in New York with Dexter and keep an eye out for Lora and the aides if any problems came up.

Okay. Max and Marybeth will have the house until July 10. Then Alison will come over with us until July 20, and then Jill and I will have through the month of August and a bit of September on our own. Perfect.

Ring! The York Theater called. Because of the very strong response to the staged reading, the producers decided they wanted to mount a full version of *Enter Laughing—The Musical,* with costumes, scenery, lights, and actors who would actually have to learn their lines.

"Great. That sounds like fun. When do we start?"

"August fifteenth for rehearsal and we'll open the first week of September."

My heart sank. "Isn't that a little early in the season?"

"That's when we can do it."

So we would have a month at the house. Not exactly our dream scenario, but we wouldn't be getting any sympathy from our friends. "Aw, you only get to stay at your house in Italy for a month. Gee, you poor guys."

We decided to throw a party for Max and Marybeth in absentia. Max knew a lot of our friends in Italy, and this way he could introduce Marybeth to everybody in one fell swoop and then, if they wanted to, they could make plans to socialize with people on their own. It would be an icebreaker. Bruce and JoJo thought it was a great idea—they never like to miss an opportunity for a party—and they said they would help organize it. We called Vittoria and hired her to do the dinner; she was all excited about meeting the kids. Then we sent out a group e-mail to the gang to settle on the best night for everybody. Jill consulted long-distance with Teresa about the table decorations and I spoke with Joe to make sure there would be enough booze. Martin and Karen insisted on bringing dessert.

It turned out to be one of the best parties I never attended. By all reports it was a blowout. Given that there were three professional photographers present, we started receiving photos over the Internet the following day— Vittoria bringing out a huge bowl of pasta; Bruno, Joe, and Michael trading off-color jokes down at the far end of the table; Marybeth in deep discussion with Sophie and Jeffrey about God knows what. Carol sent a great shot of Max making the welcoming toast to the collected throng.

"He's a younger version of you, Mike," she wrote. "And taller, of course."

Our friend Pam, who had come up from Rome to join the party, agreed. "He sat back in his chair with his wineglass and rubbed his belly—just like you do. Except that he doesn't have a belly."

Then Teresa chimed in with an e-mail and photo: "Marybeth is a younger Jill—beautiful and smart and soulful. She's a keeper."

Great party. It was as if we were there but forty years younger—and I didn't have a hangover in the morning.

The games continued when Alison, Jill, and I arrived on July 10. It was like a family tag-team match with Max and Marybeth flying west to take over the care of Dexter as we were landing in Rome to take over the task of keeping the party going.

Alessandra picked us up at the airport, and Alison sat in the front seat with her. Alessandra got a chance to work on her English.

"Alison, I promise that you will find a nice Italian man to marry you before you leave in ten days. I am positive of this."

Alison said she would hold her to the promise, and the two of them fell into a deep conversation that took us all the way to Umbria. When we passed under the aqueduct that connects Spoleto to Monteluco, Alison stopped in midsentence.

"Oh, my God, there's the . . . thing . . . that we walked across."

"The aqueduct," Jill prompted.

"Yeah. We're almost home."

"*L'aria di casa,*" said Alessandra.

"What's that?" I asked from the backseat.

"It means . . . it's hard to translate . . . but when you are in the neighborhood of your home, it's the smell, the feeling that's in the air, that is particular only to your home. It's hard to translate."

"*L'aria di casa,*" repeated Jill. "I like that. It's a nice expression."

A couple nights later, Bruce and JoJo came over to make dinner with us. Alison was eager to make fresh pasta and Bruce is a genius at it, so we decided to have a group experience. We had made a nice Bolognese sauce the night before to put over it; pasta and a simple salad would be dinner.

We cleared the marble-topped kitchen table and Bruce made two mounds of flour—one for him and one for Alison—and put two eggs next to each one. A pot of water was already simmering on the stove next to the bubbling sauce. Jill and JoJo were in the dining room, setting the table and talking away.

"You can make a two-egg pasta or a three-egg pasta—just depends on how many people you're cooking for," he said as he broke the two eggs into a well he had made in the mound of flour. Then he took a fork and started beating the eggs together as he would for scrambled eggs. Little by little, he nudged the flour into the egg until he had incorporated it into a ball of eggy dough.

"Now you do yours," he said to Alison, who started tentatively to beat the eggs together and slowly bring in the flour.

"We've got plenty of eggs and flour, so don't worry. If you screw up, we'll just do another mound."

Alison got the hang of it immediately and made a beautiful yellow ball of dough.

"Oh, she's a pro," said Bruce with admiration.

He and Alison flattened their respective balls and hand-kneaded them a bit. Then he attached the hand-crank pasta maker to the edge of the table and set the dial to the widest setting so that they could knead the dough as they sent it through. Then he started narrowing the aperture one setting at a time so that every time he sent the dough through it became thinner and thinner. At the final setting, he had a long strip of pasta about four inches wide and three feet long—so thin that you could read the newspaper through it. He set it on a towel and left the machine to Alison, who repeated the process.

After they had made enough of the sheets—forming the dough with eggs and flour, kneading it, and then rolling it out to its proper thinness—Bruce put on the pasta-cutting attachment and cranked the sheets through the machine into quarter-inch-wide strips of tagliatelle, perfect for a Bolognese. He lightly dusted them with flour and popped them into the boiling salted water, and in virtually seconds they were done and drying on towels.

Using big forks, we heaped each bowl with the freshly made pasta, sauced it with the Bolognese, tossed it together lightly, and topped it with freshly grated parmigiano.

The five of us sat down immediately and dug in. There wasn't a sound in the room as we tasted, chewed, and tasted again. The brilliance of this dish—and made correctly, it is one of the world's great eating experiences—is not so much in the sauce as in the noodles. The sauce is great—don't get me wrong; I love a good meat sauce. But the pasta—if you are lucky enough to experience it like this, scant seconds after the freshest of eggs and flour have been brought together—is a high-level sensual experience. Mix in the sauce and the cheese, and it transforms into an almost sexual experience.

After Alison went back to New York, we continued the party, but in a quieter way—small dinner parties with just us and another couple, where the talk tended to get more personal and real. And we spent a lot of time, just the two of us, hanging out at the house. The show would be going into rehearsal when we got back in a few weeks, so we started to get ourselves in shape for it. We hiked up the hill every morning and I swam laps in the pool, impressing Jill no end.

"How many laps did you do?"

"Fifty," I said smugly.

"Wow. Good for you."

I chose not to remind her that our pool is only about ten yards long.

We did vocal warm-ups every day to a tape that Jill's singing teacher made for her. We went over the lyrics to the songs in the show and worked on our scenes every day. I cooked

Michael Tucker

exclusively for Jill; this is something she likes a lot. It's also good for my waistline because her diet is mostly protein and veg—as opposed to the pasta-twice-a-day diet that I had been following religiously. So a little judicious slimming got under way, and I hoped it would make me lighter on my feet for the little bit of dancing I had to do in the show.

The Rustico became less a party house for the moment and more of what it had been back in early 1600s—a haven, a respite, a protection from the wild beasts that were prowling around in the world outside. We hunkered down, we hung pictures, baked bread, and weeded the garden, we played Scrabble at night after dinner, and when we got tired we went to bed. We breathed deeply of *l'aria di casa*—the smell and the comfort of home. Our home.

# THIRTY-ONE

# In the Wings

As THE BAND STRUCK UP THE OVERTURE on opening night, Jill waited for her entrance in the wings off stage right, and I was directly across from her in the left wings. Unseen by the audience, we bounced up and down to the catchy 1930s-style music and stretched a bit, warming up our old limbs for the opening number. We waved to each other and made faces as if to say, *Hey, look at us—we're doing a musical!*

Jill's costume and makeup, along with a dark wig with marcelled waves, couldn't hide the goyish blue-eyed beauty beneath. When Jill is happy she emanates an almost unearthly shine. You need sunglasses when she's happy.

What a year! Not one thing turned out the way I thought it would. As the putative head of household and chief prognosticator, I batted zero this year. And yet everything's fine. More than fine.

Lora has a pretty good life. She lives like Catherine the Great. She gets up when she wants, she goes to bed when she wants, she eats what she wants. If people do anything to displease her, she just hauls off and socks them. Even Jill almost had her nose broken just sitting on the couch one afternoon

*237*

reading her a poem. But this regal attitude has served Lora. She's managed to define her boundaries—probably more clearly than she ever did when she was "in her right mind"—and everyone around her tries to respect them. She's in good shape physically for a woman of eighty-nine. She's put on some weight, thanks to her granddaughter's cooking but she exercises every day, pushing her wheelchair to the park and back, squawking all the way. I suppose the squawking is good for her lungs. There are worse ways to be at eighty-nine. Being in horrible pain comes to mind.

Lora thinks she's a young girl—at least we think she thinks that. When she looks in the mirror she is always shocked to see an old face looking back at her.

"I'm not ready to die yet," she has pronounced on a few of those occasions, after getting over the surprise of her appearance. And I think that's right. I think she'll be around for a long time. Marcia thinks so as well.

"She's happy, she knows she's loved; she's not goin' anyplace."

Lora's presence and proximity have caused big changes in our family. I sometimes wonder if she's aware of that. It's impossible to tell what she knows and doesn't know, but sometimes there's a gleam in her eye that hints of a demonic plan. Whether we can credit Lora or not, both our kids have come home in both a metaphorical and a very tangible way. Not that we ever had a big rift; we've always loved and supported each other, but often from a distance. Now it seems that we seek contact; we feel better when we can see and touch one another on some sort of regular basis.

Getting to know my daughter as an adult is one of the best surprises of my life to date. As with many good things, I never knew what I was missing until I got it. Alison always prided herself on her uniqueness, which was cute when she was a kid, shocking when she was a teenager, and occasionally tedious when she was a young woman. But as an adult, now that she is wise enough to know that she is what she is—she's dazzling. I don't know many people smarter than my daughter. I find myself looking forward to the days when she's in our kitchen cooking and gabbing away with her pop. She'll drop by with Dexter and make a shopping list for Lora and the aides. Then she'll check our fridge and pantry to make sure Jill has enough yogurt and berries for her breakfast and that I have all my coffee supplies. It's not her job to cook and shop for us, but she's taken a proprietary interest in her aging parents.

"I'm making rosemary chicken for Lora tonight; should I make enough for you guys?"

"Sure."

"How about some lasagna? I could just as easily do two."

"What kind of lasagna?" I ask.

"Meat sauce with sausages."

"Uh, yeah. I'm sure someone will find some use for it."

"And I'll get Mom a fish filet that you can sauté for her?"

"Very good idea."

"And some sugar snaps? She likes them."

"Perfect."

"I'll cook them off and you can just heat them up in a little oil."

"Yes, ma'am."

We'll get into a discussion about last night's Jon Stewart or the stock market or one of Max's concerts, and then she'll go shopping, leaving me to babysit for Dexter. Every time she walks out the door, pushing her shopping cart on the way to Fairway, I feel a little buzz go up my spine, reminding me how lucky I am.

Jill and Alison are in contact every day. They've become dependent on each other in the way of best friends, and this is an achievement given their relationship and their history. From their tentative time as stepmother and stepdaughter, through the crisis of Alison's accident and her rebellious teenage years, they've now come together in a way that many mothers and daughters would envy. If Jill has something on her mind—a problem or an inspiration—she'll invariably run it by Alison. And vice versa.

Alison also has a day-to-day working relationship with Marcia and the rest of the aides and an actual professional caretaker relationship with Lora. If her grandmother doesn't like the meat loaf, Alison hears about it. And because she works closely with the aides, she has access to backstairs information and gossip that wouldn't ordinarily get to Jill.

She also knows a lot more about Max and his life than we do, but she's very circumspect with the information. She protects her brother at the same time that she leaks little bits of information that Jill and I are so hungry to hear.

"I think Max's band might get a record deal."

"What? What do you mean? What kind of record deal?"

We know absolutely nothing about the music business and we glom onto any piece of information we get and try desperately to interpret it.

"Don't tell him I said anything; it's not set yet. And he'll tell you all about it when he's ready. But I think this could really be good."

We nod optimistically, completely in the dark.

Alison is also a good friend of Marybeth. If Max is rehearsing, the two of them will often spend the evening together until he's free. Again, we—Jill especially—hunger for any piece of information about Max's romantic life, and Alison doles out choice bits to us as a dog trainer would to a pair of golden retriever puppies.

"Marybeth really gets him. You know, sometimes Max can seem like he's not really there—like he's in a coma or something? But she sees right down to who he really is. She totally gets him."

And Jill cries with joy.

Max is our spiritual adviser. Well, that's not quite right. Just say that he has a spiritual life that certainly didn't spring from the upbringing his parents gave him. Not only is he a churchgoing boy and a chanting Buddhist, but there's a spiritual element that's been central to his music ever since he began playing at age seven. His first inspiration was Mozart, with whom he completely identified, right down to the haircut. But his most powerful early influence came from the drummer Billy Higgins. When Max first saw Billy play—with Cedar Walton at Yoshi's Jazz Club in Oakland—he came home on fire.

"While he was playing, his eyes were looking up—like he was getting a message from God. The music just flowed through him—he was the messenger."

Billy Higgins had played with them all—Ornette Coleman, Dexter Gordon, Thelonious Monk. He was a pioneer of free jazz and a legend of hard bop. But it was his access to the ethereal that so impressed Max. Billy, Mozart, and Max have that in common. Then Max got a chance not only to meet Billy but to work with him at the Stanford Jazz Camp one summer. Billy sensed Max's connection with the higher spheres and became his first mentor.

Max has sought mentors throughout his professional training. When he was in the jazz program at the New School, he met Michael Carvin, the great jazz and Motown drummer, and Michael has stayed on in the role of his mentor to this day. This takes a lot of pressure off Max's dad—I can watch from the sidelines as my son becomes his own man and an artist of his own unique stamp. If anything, particularly in the area of being an artist, the son is mentor to the father.

That brings me to me. I've had some turnarounds this year that I didn't see coming, the first being my attitude toward acting. I thought I was pretty much done with it. I had taken my pension and had my sights set on our life in Italy, but a couple of things turned my head around again. First was Jill's ongoing, dogged insistence on examining herself and on making herself whole. I couldn't live in intimate proximity to that and not be affected. Her persistent delving forced me to take my old crusty, rusted delver out of mothballs; I went back to therapy. And there I discovered—among other things—that at least half of my motivation for the stage was from old, childhood crap: pleasing my mother, in short, so that she wouldn't go off the deep end. The other half was for myself. So, slowly and with help, I'm eighty-sixing the old stuff and starting to act for my own pleasure only, and of course I'm having a ball. It also didn't hurt that the director and writer of the show gave me a song to sing this time—a song-and-dance number with another actor that's exhilarating to do every night. So, acting is fun now.

This year also taught me—or reminded me—that having a good life has nothing to do with making it happen my way. What is, is; start with that and not with how you want things to be. Once you get that part, the trick is to like what you have. It doesn't matter if Jill and I are eating pork chops in Italy or Jell-O mold in Santa Barbara, it doesn't matter if we're harvesting our olive trees or strutting our stuff onstage, it doesn't matter if we're riding on the back of an ostrich. All that matters is that she continues to tolerate my being next to her and at night lets me crawl in beside her. That's all. With that I can manage to face anything the world wants to dish out.

Jill? Well, I've already told you about her year. It's amazing to me that a person can be so unbendable and so bendable at the same time. How does she do that? How can she be so rigid and so malleable? So forceful and so yielding? Maybe the answer lies in the mother thing. It usually does—we all have mothers. Except for a few drama critics, perhaps. And our mothers occupy a unique vantage point in the drama of our lives. They have house seats—and even though they've seen it all in the rehearsals, they don't miss a single nuance of the performance. Our mothers are watching us even when they're not watching us. My mother is watching me and she's been dead for eight years.

One of our gurus in northern California talked about how some people "hex" us. As he defined it, a hex is like a trip down Insecurity Lane. Say there's something that you know to be true, deep down inside, but you've devised a way to deny it. A hex happens when people put it back in your face. And they don't even have to be aware of you to do it. An ambitious coworker is hexing you about your lack of ambition whether he knows you're there or not. And the greatest hex of all, our guru told us, is like a rusted old harpoon plunged right into your heart—and there's a little tag dangling off the handle that says, "Love, Mom."

Jill has pulled a hat trick. She not only has a mother, she is a mother—of two grown children, and on top of that, she's had to be a mother to *her* mother most of her life. Do we really need to wonder why she's complicated?

Oops, there's our cue; here we go. We'll sing and dance our way through the next two hours and then I'll be sitting at P. J. Clarke's in front of a burger and a big glass of wine. Here we go.

# Acknowledgments

Thanks to my agents at Dystel & Goderich Literary Management. Jane and Miriam are the best one-two punch a writer could have. Thanks also to everyone at Grove/Atlantic—Morgan Entrekin, Eric Price, Andrew Robinton, Charles Woods, Deb Seager, to single out a few. I'm proud to be associated with this great independent publisher. Lastly, I'd like to thank my family—Jill, of course, Alison and Max, and especially Lora Fern Longanecker Eikenberry Collins, who brought us all together.